ENGLISH CASTLES EXPLAINED

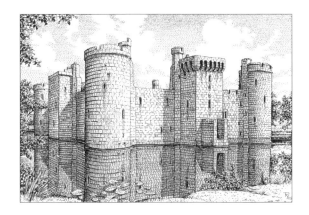

— TREVOR YORKE —

COUNTRYSIDE BOOKS
NEWBURY BERKSHIRE

First published 2003
© Trevor Yorke 2003
Reprinted 2005, 2014

COUNTRYSIDE BOOKS
3 Catherine Road
Newbury, Berkshire

To view our complete range of books,
please visit us at
www.countrysidebooks.co.uk

ISBN 978 1 85306 819 5

Photographs and illustrations by the author

Produced through The Letterworks Ltd., Reading
Printed by Berforts Information Press, Oxford

CONTENTS

Introduction

The English medieval castle conjures up distinct images in our mind. To some it is a picture of a Chivalrous Age with gallant knights, noble lords and faithful peasants set among the imposing battlements and towers of a graceful fortification. To others it may be the noise and smell of battle with stone missiles crashing into walls, scaling ladders erected through a hail of arrows, and battering rams smashing huge oak gates while burning hot liquid pours from above. The younger folk probably think of running along hidden passages, up spiral staircases and down into the dank and dark dungeons! Others may just think of those castles they have visited and imagine the craggy walls forming a dramatic skyline along the crest of a hill, or towering gatehouses reflecting in the tranquil waters of the surrounding moat.

I have often found the understanding of these fragmented remains is frustratingly elusive. There are books written by

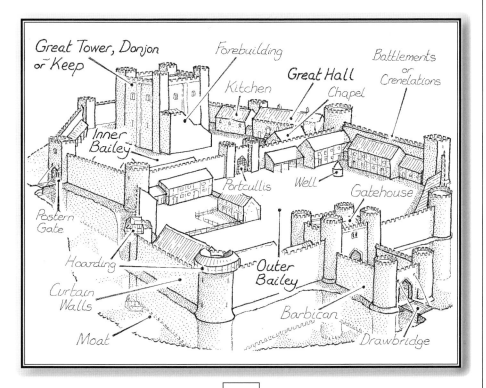

enthusiasts and experts on the subject, others which pack in beautiful photographs, and also plenty of imaginative publications for children. I find, though, that many are either too intense and get bogged down with technical and historic details, or are too lightweight, leaving questions unanswered and the features I see unexplained. It is with the intention of plugging the gap between too much information and too little that this series of books was born.

The first thing I learnt about the true medieval castle is that it was both a military base and a palatial home for its owner. These dual roles make it unique in English architecture and shape the format of this book. It is also worth noting that unlike abbeys, churches and cathedrals, which generally follow distinct layouts and periodic styles, the castle was shaped by its site, its owner's aspirations and its location within the country. So although certain details will be assigned to a period, or a type of fortification will be dated, these can only be a general guide as you will always find exceptions to the rule, this individuality being one of the great attractions of castles.

The book is broken down into three sections. The first charts the castle's origins, its development through the Middle Ages and its subsequent decline, with chapters describing the national events, the role of the castle and the styles of fortification in each period. They each include a collection of pictures illustrating the features you can still see today, together with a drawing of a mock castle, called 'Exemplar Castle'. This illustration is intended to show the development of the castle through the ages. The second section looks at the individual parts of a castle, from military features like the portcullis and murder holes to the imposing halls and decorated chapels of its domestic side. It also includes some surprising elements like medieval toilets, gardens and tournament sites. The third section contains a glossary to explain any unfamiliar terms that may have crept in and a time chart to act as a quick guide for dating castles.

I hope you find the book an attractive way of discovering what the ruined structures you see today originally looked like, and that it enhances your next visit to a castle. Perhaps you will even be able to impress your bemused companions by informing them that the arch you have just passed under looks 12th century to you!

Trevor Yorke

SECTION

I

THE HISTORY

OF

ENGLISH CASTLES

CHAPTER 1

The Origins of Castles

FIG 1.1: PEVERIL CASTLE AND MAM TOR, DERBYSHIRE: *The lines along the ridge of the hill in the background with the concave landslip are from an Iron Age hillfort, built to protect a settlement within. The castle walls in the foreground, however, were built by the local lord some 1,500 years later as part of a defended home and military base from which his estate below could be patrolled. Although some hillforts are known today as castles, we will be focusing on the true medieval structures which uniquely filled this dual role of home and garrison.*

What is a Castle?

Before looking for its origins it is important to define what exactly we mean by a castle – and just as crucially what it is not. An arrangement of towers, battlements, earthworks and gateways does not automatically constitute a castle, for these elements have all been used before and since in other types of

FIG 1.2: DUN CARLOWAY BROCH, ISLE OF LEWIS: *The remains of a circular broch exposing its hollow walls between which stairs were built and a central area accessible through the low doorway to the front.*

fortifications and buildings.

Iron Age man dug ditches, raised banks mounted with wooden fences and formed complicated defensive gateways around the tops of prominent hills up to 1,700 years before castle moats and palisades were erected by invading Normans. They were a place of defence for a community and any attackers were usually repelled by men standing outside the perimeter fence.

The remains of about five hundred circular stone towers are dotted through the north and west of Scotland, many of them pre-dating the castle by at least a thousand years. These brochs were strongholds with a guarded narrow entrance, stairs rising through hollow walls, and timber platforms within the central area, similar to the medieval castle tower. The Romans constructed forts in towns, along Hadrian's Wall and around the south and east coast of England. These featured stone walls with battlements and powerful gateways protected by round towers, again much in common with our idea of a castle. Since the medieval period many lords have built new, so-called castles which, despite having imposing façades and often being sited upon an earlier fortification, are exposed as shams by their large window openings filled with glass, arrangements of towers designed to please the eye, and surrounding gardens rather than defensive earthworks.

Despite appearances the above examples are not castles, although to add to the confusion many are referred to as such, like Maiden Castle which is an Iron Age hill fort! The type that we will be focusing on is the true medieval castle. They differ from these other structures in that they fulfilled a dual role as both the home of a king, baron or his tenant and as a fortification from which to attack or defend his estates. These imposing structures reflected the power and authority of those who built them and were local centres of government and justice. They were also an important element of the social structure known today as the feudal system. So it is in the origins of feudalism that we find the first castles.

Feudalism

Not since the Roman Empire had collapsed in the 5th century had one man ruled such a large part of mainland Europe. The year was AD 800 and the man was Charles, King of the Franks, better known to history as Charlemagne. His empire spread across modern day France, Germany, Austria and down into Italy. To manage such a large territory he broke the land down into counties with nobles to defend and govern them. In return for this land a noble would be expected to provide armed men at a time of war. Charlemagne, in common with most rulers through the Middle Ages, had no standing army.

Another habit inherited from their Germanic past was for the Franks to split the lands amongst their sons when they died. Although Charlemagne had only one surviving son, Louis, he in turn had three competitive heirs who divided the Empire three ways in AD 843, breaking down central government and heralding a century of civil unrest. Not only did these kings have to tackle the problem of lesser nobles gaining too much power over their territories but they also had to face up to new external threats from the Magyars, the Saracens and in particular the Vikings.

With their fast moving ships which could proceed upriver, the Vikings could strike quickly far inland. The Franks, though, had developed a secret weapon, the stirrup. This gave the horse rider a firm footing so that, when he charged, his and the animal's weight was behind the lance, which was more effective than just throwing it. Hence the armoured soldier on horseback, or knight, was born, allowing for the formation of local cavalry forces that could respond quickly to any invader.

The feudal system developed alongside these military changes in order to physically and financially support them. Although it varied in structure, it basically formed a pyramid shaped social order with the king at the top. Below him were the vassals, a class of professional fighting men who often developed into troublesome local aristocrats, knights who might hold an estate or manor of their own, and farmers and peasants who gave up former types of land holding to fall under the protection of this system. Each level would receive an amount of land from the one above, and in return would provide services and produce to their superior. This arrangement was crucial to the knight for it provided him with an income and the manpower that he needed for training, armour, equipment and horses. Being a medieval knight was an expensive occupation!

For the feudal system to work the kings, dukes, counts and their vassals required local bases, which would be a home from which to administer and oversee their territory yet at the same time a garrison to house and equip their forces. These would not be large army forts which could be defended by thousands of soldiers, but more numerous local defensive structures which would have to resist attack with a smaller number of men.

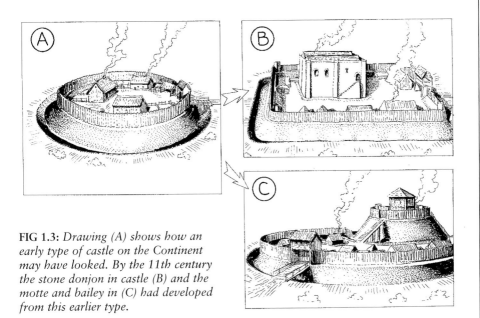

FIG 1.3: *Drawing (A) shows how an early type of castle on the Continent may have looked. By the 11th century the stone donjon in castle (B) and the motte and bailey in (C) had developed from this earlier type.*

The First Castles

The first fortifications built by the competing local lords were probably no more than a ditch and bank, topped by a palisade erected around their halls and ancillary buildings. The earth dug from the outer ditch was conveniently pushed up inside to make the bank, making the slope which confronted any attacker even more formidable. At some point a watch tower could have been added to guard a crucial river crossing or important trading centre where castles were usually strategically placed. These may have developed earthen ramps around their bases to protect their lower parts from fire and to gain height. Another change which may have occurred was for the lord's hall to be isolated in its own defensive area, separate from the ancillary buildings within their own fortification.

Although the Viking threat was used as a reason for building these early castles, the real motivation of the nobles was probably competition with their neighbours. To possess a stronger, more advanced castle enabled the noble to hold on to or invade neighbouring lands. By the middle of the 11th century two types of fortification had evolved. An enclosure castle which contained a large building called a donjon within a surrounding bank and palisade (fig 1.3B) and a motte and bailey castle which had a watch tower fully elevated upon a mound with a separate enclosed area below (fig 1.3C). Both of these types were built by the invading Normans in England after 1066 and therefore will be explained in detail in the next chapter.

While the Old Frankish kingdom disintegrated into localised infighting, across the Channel in Saxon England the threat from Vikings had a different effect. In the late 9th century the Vikings, in this

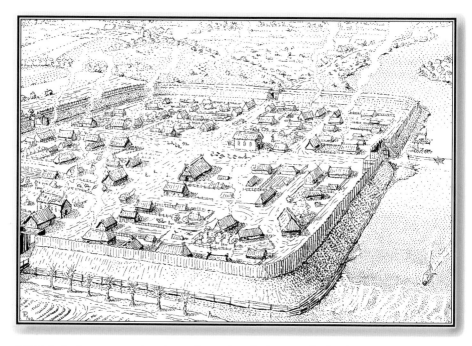

FIG 1.4: *A view over an imaginary Saxon burgh showing the bank with a ditch outside and the gravel-surfaced roads crossing in the middle. A road also runs around the inside of the bank to permit easy access to any part of the defences at time of trouble.*

case from Denmark (known as Danes), began to settle in England. They were looking to settle rather than just pillage and would have almost overrun the country were it not for stout resistance from Alfred, the King of Wessex. As a result the country was split diagonally in two, and to reinforce the boundary of Alfred's southern and western region he established fortified towns called burghs, with earth banks and ditches surrounding the settlements. These were the nearest the Saxons came to building a castle but, like the hillforts of the Iron Age, they were communal defences and were not personal structures for overseeing an estate.

While Danes were colonising the east and north of England, another Viking group from Scandinavia had become such a force on the other side of the Channel that the then king of the Old West Frankish kingdom (soon to become France) had granted them and their leader, Rollo, a territory around Rouen in AD 911. They quickly expanded their lands and became the Dukes of Normandy, losing their Viking connections and becoming embroiled in the politics and infighting of this part of Northern France.

By the mid 11th century there were also growing associations across the Channel with England. Edward the Confessor had been brought up within the court of Duke Robert I and his bastard son, William, who inherited Normandy from Robert in 1035. When Edward took the English throne in 1042 he even invited a number of Normans to join his court and may have promised the crown to William upon his death. Duke William at the time was busy suppressing the barons (his feudal vassals) who threatened his power with their own castles erected without the Duke's permission. No doubt he thought at the time: 'If only I could wipe the slate clean and start again I would know how to reorganise this country of mine!' The opportunity to do exactly that would soon arise. When Edward the Confessor died, Harold Goodwinson, the most powerful man in the country, seized the English throne. Upon hearing the news, Duke

William set about building and acquiring boats for his invasion force to conquer England. It was 1066.

FIG 1.5: EXEMPLAR CASTLE: *Our first visit to the site of our imaginary castle shows Exemplar Village developing around a crossroads beside an important river crossing. It has grown up partly within old defensive earthworks from an earlier time and you can just make out their banks and ditches in the bottom right corner by the church and then swinging round at the back between the houses and the river. The village is the principal one within a large estate, and acts as a trading centre and home to a Saxon noble complete with his hall and church.*

FIG 1.5: *A typical village c. 1050*

CHAPTER 2

The Conquest and the Norman Kings 1066-1135

FIG 2.1: THE TOWER OF LONDON: *This famous royal fortress has expanded over many centuries to its present size but at its core is the White Tower from which the complex is named. This stone donjon, or keep, in the picture above was begun in 1078 within a small fortification which William the Conqueror had established in the south-east corner of London's old Roman walls a few years earlier. Although it has retained its original proportions, the exterior finish, most windows and the caps upon the towers are all from a later date (only the four double windows on the top level, near centre, are original). In the 13th century the walls were whitewashed, hence the name White Tower.*

FIG 2.2: BERKHAMSTED CASTLE, HERTFORDSHIRE: *It was at Berkhamsted, 28 miles north-east of London, that William the Conqueror received a delegation from the capital who invited him to take the crown. Afterwards a castle was erected here for the king's half brother, the large mound or motte in the middle of the picture being from this original fortification. It would have had a timber tower and circular wall upon its top although trees have now invaded its once impregnable slopes. The open ground in front, called the bailey, would have contained buildings and workshops and would have been a noisy hive of activity. In the mid 12th century the castle was rebuilt in stone (the flint walls in the foreground) by its then owner Thomas à Becket, although these walls were later breached by Prince Louis of France in 1216 during a little known French invasion of our shores.*

William, Duke of Normandy had some degree of luck on his side at the Battle of Hastings. King Harold had been forced to march his army to Stamford Bridge, near York, to defeat an invasion led by his brother Tostig and the Norwegian king and then had to race back down to Sussex in only a matter of days.

After his victory Duke William took a meandering route through south-east England and around the west of London, establishing a number of castles on his way, until at Berkhamsted in Hertfordshire he was finally offered the crown by the remaining Saxon nobles. He spent much of the next five years suppressing revolts around the countryside and establishing castles in the county towns as local power bases. There are a number of accounts of rebels taking a town but being unable to break the castle's defences.

Although William retained much of the Saxon local government he did replace it in Sussex with 'rapes', strips of land based around castles, initially at Pevensey, Hastings, Lewes and Arundel, each designed to protect his communication with Normandy. In the turbulent border regions he grouped estates together into earldoms and granted them to his most trusted followers. William is also credited with introducing the feudal system although the Saxons already had some elements of this Continental social order. However, now Saxon kings, earls and thegns were replaced by Norman kings, barons and knights. In William's new order, vassals owed to their superior a certain number of days (around 40 per year) to guard his castle and fight his battles (Knights' Service or Castle Guard).

By the time of his death in 1087 William had established castles from Chester in the west to Norwich in the east and from Exeter in the south to Newcastle in the north. Although the Domesday Book records 49 castles, it is likely that the figure at this time was nearer 80 to 90. These castles were hated symbols of Norman suppression; the Saxons not only had to help build them but also found many of their homes flattened by their construction (some 166 houses in Lincoln for instance). To the Norman conquerors the castle was vital in enabling a small garrison of men to hold power over a wide tract of land. They probably numbered around 25,000, in a country with a Saxon population of over a million.

Another great change brought about by William was the transference of estates from Saxon to Norman hands. He had forged his army on the promise of land as well as riches, so the barons who fought with him now expected territories to add to their possessions back in France. The new king divided his kingdom again, granting his faithful followers estates, grouped together to form an 'honour'. One estate would usually be selected by the baron as his principal holding or 'caput' and it is here he would erect his own castle, with economic as much as military strategy in mind when choosing

FIG 2.3: *An imaginary map showing how William scattered his vassals' estates so their power was not concentrated in one area. The barons (labelled A-G) selected one as their principal estate. For instance, Baron A has chosen an estate at the mouth of a river because it contains a successful port rather than picking the largest or most central one which would have been strategically better to control his lands. Here, he built his castle sited due to local economics rather than military planning.*

its site. So that they would not become powerful enough to threaten his position as they had done in Normandy, William endeavoured to make sure their lands were scattered to prevent them dominating a region. He also made sure that his barons could not erect a castle without his permission, and under his powerful and ruthless rule he was generally successful at this, unlike some who were to follow him.

William II continued his father's work of consolidation and expansion, taking over Cumberland and Westmorland which had previously been under Scottish rule and establishing a castle at Carlisle. His reign, though, was disrupted by rebellion, mainly from Norman supporters of his elder brother Robert who had been given Normandy (that Frankish habit of splitting a kingdom between heirs yet again causing trouble). After William's suspicious death in a hunting accident in 1100, he was succeeded by the Conqueror's youngest son Henry, who turned much of his attention to matters of law. Under him a shift from Sussex to Hampshire and Dorset as a point of embarkation to the Continent resulted in new castles being erected at sites such as Corfe and Carisbrooke.

Castle Types
🟦 MOTTE AND BAILEY

The most popular type of Norman castle was the motte and bailey. It comprised the motte, a conical shaped earthwork, and a bailey, the enclosure which was surrounded by a bank and wooden palisade. At the time of the Conquest they were a relatively recent development in castle design. The speed with which they could be erected, and the powerful position they offered with only the use of

earthworks and timber fencing must have played a part in their popularity.

The motte is not simply a mound of earth. It was carefully constructed from layers of materials - chalk, sand, flint, rock and gravel as well as the soil thrown up from the V-shaped ditch dug around its base. The sloping sides could have been finished off with a crust of clay or wooden boards while the flat top could be reinforced with hardcore or timber piles. Although some may have used existing mounds like old barrows or natural rock outcrops, the fact that many have survived a thousand years after they were raised is testament to their surprisingly complicated construction methods, even though some were erected in only a matter of weeks!

The purpose of the motte was to support a watch tower, usually referred to at the time as a donjon. Unfortunately none of these timber towers survive and their appearance can only be guessed at from the post holes they left and contemporary illustrations, as in the Bayeux Tapestry. On a few the tower may have been a simple building raised on posts so that the defenders could pass underneath giving more room on the congested top, while on more important castles it could have been a three or four floored elaborate structure with hall, chamber and storerooms within. Around the perimeter of the crest of the motte a timber palisade, possibly with towers, would have acted as a refuge from which defenders could bombard soldiers trying to climb up its steep and often slippery slopes. This arrangement of tower and palisade acted as the last retreat for the castle inhabitants when under attack and was often positioned to the side of the bailey so if all was lost a quick escape could be made down the outer face of the motte.

The bailey would have contained the

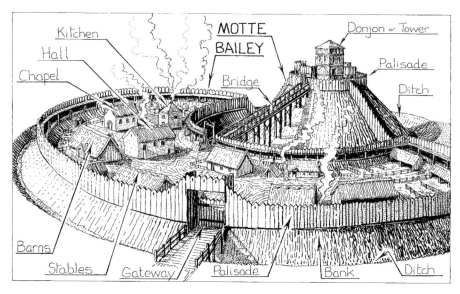

Kitchen

Hall

Chapel

MOTTE

BAILEY

Bridge

Donjon or Tower

Palisade

Ditch

Barns

Stables

Gateway

Palisade

Bank

Ditch

FIG 2.4: *A view of an imaginary motte and bailey castle.*

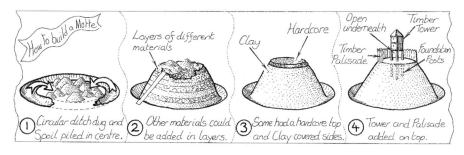

How to build a Motte

Layers of different materials

Clay

Hardcore

Open underneath

Timber Tower

Timber Palisade

Foundation Posts

① Circular ditch dug and Spoil piled in centre. ② Other materials could be added in layers. ③ Some had a hardcore top and Clay covered sides. ④ Tower and Palisade added on top.

FIG 2.5: *A diagram showing how a motte may have been constructed (the composition of the mound would have varied depending on the local geology).*

lord's main hall, the chapel, kitchen, stables, forges and stores. It too would be surrounded by a bank, raised from the soil dug out from the ditch on its outside and surmounted by a timber palisade. The ditch or moat could be dry or wet, in the latter case sometimes with only a few feet of water in the bottom, which was sufficient to make the climbing of its sides treacherous. There

were many variations in the positioning of the motte and bailey. In some the gap between them was spanned by a thin bridge while in others steps sufficed.

Motte and bailey castles were ideal for the rapid suppression of the Saxon population which William and his barons required. In the long term the limitation of building on top of the motte and the changes in military design meant that they were either abandoned or incorporated into stone castles which have overwhelmed their simple origins.

◙ RINGWORK CASTLES

It is likely that some three-quarters of Norman Castles were of the motte and bailey type. The majority of the remaining were of a more simple design with the owner's buildings contained within a fortified enclosure; today these are often referred to as ringworks. They were frequently built using existing earthworks.

Ringwork castles leave less distinctive remains than a motte and bailey. Many were quickly erected after the Conquest since they could hold the king's or baron's knights close together, and their ring of ditch and bank could be easily manned. As the Normans' hold over the country became secure and these knights spread out to their own manors, the castle would have to be defended by a smaller number of soldiers, so a motte or great tower was often erected within the enclosure as a strong point. Most of these earliest

enclosure type castles that survive will be found with later keeps or stone walls, both of which will be discussed in later chapters.

◙ GREAT TOWERS

Although in the early phases of the Norman Conquest castles were built rapidly and without long-term survival in mind, some did feature stone walls and buildings, the most notable of which were the great towers, later referred to as keeps. Although stone keeps will be discussed in detail in the next chapter (most date from the 12th century) there are a number from this period, the most notable being the Tower of London (see fig 2.1) and Colchester Castle. These great structures were built within old Roman fortifications, and at the latter site brick and stone from the 600 year old ruins were reused to save time and money (see fig 2.10).

They are notable for the apse that breaks their otherwise square plan. These contain the end of the chapel with the altar (chancel) and were common features on Norman churches, although few survive today.

FIG 2.6: COLCHESTER CASTLE, ESSEX: *Another of the earliest stone keeps which was started in 1085 and is very similar to its contemporary, the White Tower (fig 2.1). Note the distinctive semi circular protrusion that held the altar of the castle chapel and the four towers in each corner. The castle was taller when built, its upper storeys having been removed and the windows and round tower added in the 18th century.*

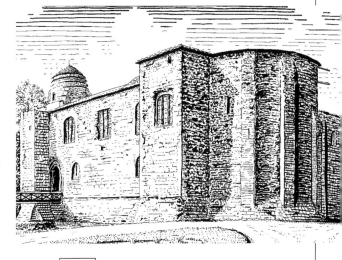

FIG 2.7: SHERBORNE OLD CASTLE, DORSET: *The gateway of a stone castle built by the Bishop of Salisbury, Roger of Caen, in the early 12th century. Note the shallow buttresses running up the corners, a common Norman feature. At this time the lifting drawbridge had not been developed, so the stone piers that you can still see emerging from the moat supported a fixed bridge with removable planks which could be lifted at the time of attack. The two upper windows were inserted by Sir Walter Raleigh in the 16th century long after it fulfilled any military purpose.*

▣ BISHOPS' CASTLES

In addition to the king and his barons, bishops were also great castle builders in the late 11th and early 12th century. Although today we would be horrified if the Archbishop of Canterbury had his own tank regiment, in this period many clerics came from a warfaring background, and as sons of the nobility they were educated in swordsmanship rather than the reading of scriptures. As the Church held about one quarter of the land in the country, it too had to supply knights for the king as part of its feudal duty, and hence required military bases. Some, like the Bishop of Salisbury, became the richest men in the country and built grand castles with stone curtain walls, gatehouses, towers and courtyard houses, more palaces than fortifications.

These clerics were among the few in England who were literate and numerate, and with their experience of building stone churches they made ideal candidates to design and oversee the king's major castle building projects. (Bishop Gundulf of Rochester was responsible for the White Tower in fig 2.1.)

FIG 2.9: EXEMPLAR CASTLE: *The Norman Conquest has led to great changes in Exemplar Village. The Saxon peasantry now have a new lord, a Norman baron, who has chosen this estate as the centre of his honour and has erected a motte and bailey castle within the old circular earthworks. In the bottom left corner a timber tower stands upon the motte and commands a view over the fortified bailey below, and the village and river crossing beyond. The parish church in the bottom right corner (as opposed to the lord's personal chapel within the bailey) has been enlarged with a circular ended chancel or apse erected upon its eastern end.*

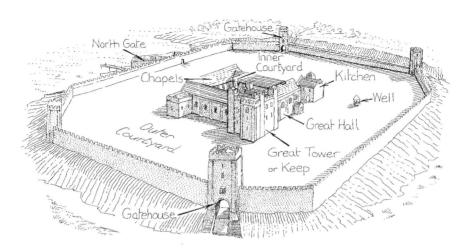

FIG 2.8: SHERBORNE OLD CASTLE, DORSET: *An aerial view over the castle as it may have appeared when originally built in the early 12th century. The outer courtyard would have probably contained workshops, storehouses and some form of kitchen garden. Its rectangular shape with angled corners is unusual at this early date and differs from later ones in only having a few towers along its course. Enclosure castles of the 13th and 14th century have only short lengths of wall between numerous towers and these are referred to as curtain walls (see fig 4.6).*

FIG 2.9

STILL OUT THERE

FIG 2.10: COLCHESTER CASTLE, ESSEX: *A section of the wall showing two shallow vertical buttresses running up the wall which were a common feature of Norman stone keeps (also see figs 2.1 and 2.6) The angled out plinth (lowest section of wall) is another distinctive characteristic.*

FIG 2.11: PILSBURY HILLS, DERBYSHIRE: *The remains of motte and bailey castles are one of the most distinctive types of earthworks that can still be seen today across the country. They consist of a grass mound, usually rounded off and lower than when built, with one or two enclosures formed by a bank and ditch to the side of it or completely enclosing the mound. The photograph here shows one such example in a remote valley of the Peak District, with the motte covered in small trees just left of centre. To each side and just in front of it are two oval shaped baileys, the left hand*

one only half in the picture, while the right hand enclosure has the rocky outcrop by the tall tree forming its eastern edge. The drawing to the side shows the simple outline of its original form.

FIG 2.12: COLCHESTER CASTLE, ESSEX: *A detail from this early stone keep showing Roman bricks (they are the flat tile-shaped blocks stacked up in the left corner and running in horizontal bands through the rough stonework).*

FIG 2.13: KENILWORTH CASTLE, WARWICKSHIRE: *An example of a Norman window from the inside of the keep looking out. Most openings on the outside of a castle would have originally been little more than slits, especially on the lower storeys. Larger windows would have been a defensive nightmare and where they appear they usually date from post medieval times when the castle was used as a residence.*

FIG 2.14: PEVERIL CASTLE, DERBYSHIRE: *A section of wall showing how some stones have been laid in a zig-zag form between horizontal ones in what is known as a herringbone pattern. This was commonly used in late Saxon and Norman construction.*

CHAPTER 3

Civil War and the Angevin Kings 1135–1215

FIG 3.1: PEVERIL CASTLE, DERBYSHIRE: *Known in the Middle Ages as the 'Castle of the Peak', it was begun soon after the Conquest with stone walls enclosing a triangular shaped area on top of dramatic cliffs (see fig 2.14). After the civil war of King Stephen's reign the owner, William Peveril, withdrew from direct action with Henry II and left the castle to the king to spend his days in a monastery. Henry is credited with building the stone keep in this picture which was small by the standards of the day with only one main room above the basement. It was positioned next to the then gateway with the upper third of its walls protecting a pointed roof while the spiral stairs on the left side mark the entrance to the interior (originally with a wooden staircase).*

A Brief History

On a November night in 1120 a ship sailing back to England from Normandy, allegedly with a drunken crew, sank with the loss of most on board. Crucially one of the passengers was Prince William, the only son of Henry I and heir to the throne. This tragedy, known as the 'White Ship Disaster', threw the King into turmoil and he spent the remaining fifteen years of his reign trying to establish a successor.

There were two candidates for the throne. The first was Henry's daughter Matilda (referred to as the Empress due to a previous marriage to the Holy Roman Emperor), to whom the barons had sworn allegiance should the King have no son. The second was Stephen, Henry's nephew, who the King may have favoured, especially as he was in dispute with his daughter around the time of his death. In a period when leadership in battle was a prime requirement of a ruler, a male was always preferred, and most magnates switched their allegiance to Stephen upon Henry's death in 1135.

Unlike his predecessors, Stephen did not possess the ruthlessness required of a 12th-century king, and his lack of central control enabled the barons to do as they liked, and they liked very much to fight their neighbours and build castles. Stephen's position was made worse by the ongoing battle for the throne with Matilda which plunged the country into a 14-year civil war. The Empress Matilda's second marriage was to Geoffrey, Count of Anjou, nicknamed 'Plantagenet', it is believed, after the sprig of broom (*planta genista*) that he reputedly wore in his cap. While her husband conquered Normandy, Matilda battled with Stephen, capturing him after the Battle of Lincoln in 1141 but losing the initiative due to a lack of political tact. Accepting that she would never be queen, Matilda pursued the claim of her son Henry, one which Stephen reluctantly had to recognise shortly before his death in 1154.

The new king, Henry II, was one of our great monarchs. He established his authority and demolished the illegal castles which the barons had erected without royal permission in the preceding 14 years of anarchy. He also expanded the lands of his family, the Angevins, establishing an empire that covered most of western France as well as England.

Richard the Lionheart succeeded his father in 1189 and spent barely four months of his ten year reign in England. His brother John was an even worse ruler, losing most of his father's hard fought gains, entering into civil war with his barons and ending his reign at Newark as a result of dysentery contracted after getting stuck in the mud while crossing the Wash.

The Castle in this Period

Throughout these eventful times castles played an important part in battles for control of the realm. A notable example is when in 1140 King Stephen laid siege to Oxford Castle with the Empress Matilda trapped within. She made a daring escape, being lowered from the walls at night, dressed in white as camouflage against the snowbound countryside. She then headed south to take refuge in Wallingford Castle where the pursuing King went to the effort of erecting a siege castle on the opposite bank of the Thames. The ability of a king to break into a castle was crucial in this period and Henry II was regarded as a powerful monarch partly from his reputation for destroying the mightiest fortifications. He used a team of experts in siege warfare who were skilled at burning down timberwork, mining under stone walls and constructing ever more effective throwing machines (see chapter

To hold out against such an effective attack, castles would now have to be stronger, with stone structures and walls a virtual must (although in a few cases stone buildings were still surrounded by timber palisades).

The 12th century found the Normans established and settled in their new English possessions and the castle played a central role in this system. Increased political and military demands made the castles of the late 12th century more expensive, so that only the king and the greatest barons could afford to upgrade and garrison them. Hence the overall number starts to decline from 1,000 or so at the end of Stephen's reign to only around 300 by 1215.

Castle Types

A spate of castle building on new sites occurred with the loss of central control during the civil war of Stephen's reign. The remains of hundreds of earthwork fortifications across the country today date from these turbulent times, when motte and bailey or ringwork castles were quickly erected in timber and earth by land-grabbing barons. Some castles lasted only a few years; one was even demolished before it was finished, while most were rendered unusable, taken over by the Crown or returned upon a hefty fine when Henry II re-established royal authority after 1154. The strength of defence that could be achieved in a short time without specialist workers and expensive materials had made the motte and bailey castle an ideal tool at a time of war or invasion.

▧ SHELL KEEPS

Norman builders did not trust the motte to take the increased weight of a large stone building, so the small tower that stood upon its crown could not simply be superseded by a larger stone keep. One

FIG 3.2: ST GEORGE'S TOWER, OXFORD CASTLE: *A late 11th/early 12th century tower built in the outer wall of Oxford Castle, from which the Empress Matilda possibly made her daring escape.*

8). When King John was in dispute with his barons, the major events were centred around sieges of castles rather than battles in open fields. At Rochester one of the barons, William de Albini, had taken the castle only for a furious King to lay siege to it. Using his team of miners, King John brought down the south-east tower of its massive keep. The gap was later repaired with a round tower, which today contrasts with the earlier square ones in the other corners.

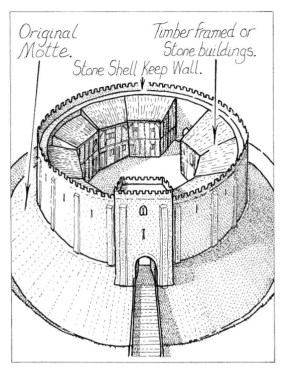

Original Motte.

Stone Shell Keep Wall.

Timber framed or Stone buildings.

FIG 3.3: *A view of a shell keep.*

FIG 3.4: ARUNDEL CASTLE, SUSSEX: *The 12th century shell keep on top of the grass motte can be seen curving away to the left of the picture. The entrance tower in the front was a 13th century addition with access originally through a door to the right of it.*

solution was to replace the timber palisade that ran around the circumference of the top with a stone wall and then construct timber buildings within, which would lean up against the inside of the wall. This lighter construction also had the advantage of having its walls out of reach of miners so they could be thinner than those of a stone keep, which further helped reduce the overall weight.

 GREAT TOWERS, DONJONS OR KEEPS

The most notable feature added to castles during the 12th century, replacing the motte as the prominent strong point, was the great tower, or donjon. This not only met the demands of the latest military technology but could also provide improved accommodation for the lord or his constable. Keeps were erected in both ringwork and motte and bailey castles, in the case of the later sometimes by flattening the old mound and building on top of it (see fig 3.12). It was fashionable in the 12th century for them to be sited at the weakest point in the defences, which was the entrance, hence many keeps are found near, or are a part of, the castle gateway.

Most keeps were rectangular or square in plan and from two to five storeys high. Walls were up to 20 ft thick in order to withstand direct hits from missiles, although passages and small rooms which

FIG 3.5: RICHMOND CASTLE, NORTH YORKSHIRE: *This towering keep was built over the original entrance to the castle in the mid 12th century to strengthen this weak point, with a new gateway positioned to the right (the rectangular block in the photograph is a 19th century replacement). Note the round arch at the bottom and how the wall buttresses start from above this level showing that the base of the keep on this side was part of the original gateway.*

were set within them could prove a weaker point for an accurate projectile. Their imposing height also made the walls less likely to be scaled by attackers, while their stone construction reduced the fire risk (timber roofs, floors and doorways were still vulnerable though). Like the early examples mentioned in the last chapter, they had a basement at ground level and an entrance on the first floor which was accessed via external stairs. A popular improvement was to enclose these within a forebuilding which added further barriers to any would-be attacker as well as creating additional rooms, usually a vestibule through which you would enter, and perhaps a chapel above this. Most forebuildings have since been removed, although their stone foundations often remain on one side of the keep (see fig 3.13). On the first floor or higher would be the hall and above or to the side of this the private chamber of the owner. The hall would often be two storeys high, sometimes with a mural gallery overlooking events. Service and storage rooms could occupy the lower floors, a corner tower or even be in chambers within the wall itself.

FIG 3.6: *Three types of keep.*

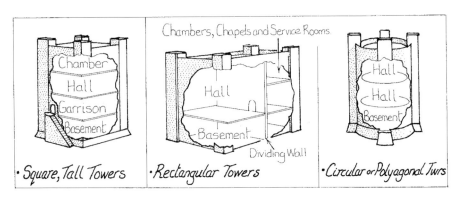

Chambers, Chapels and Service Rooms

• *Square, Tall Towers*   • *Rectangular Towers*   • *Circular or Polyagonal Twrs*

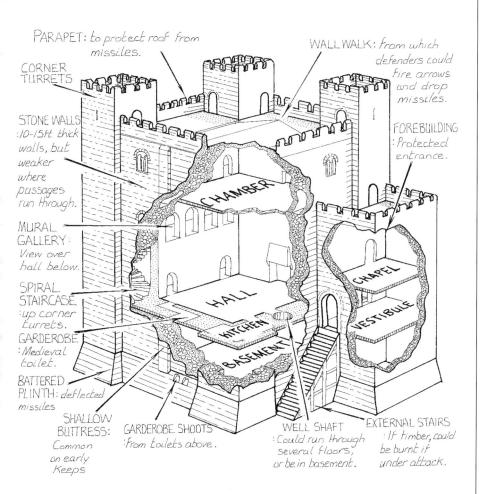

PARAPET: to protect roof from missiles.

CORNER TURRETS

STONE WALLS :10-15ft thick walls, but weaker where passages run through.

MURAL GALLERY: View over hall below.

SPIRAL STAIRCASE :up corner turrets.

GARDEROBE : Medieval toilet.

BATTERED PLINTH: deflected missiles

SHALLOW BUTTRESS: Common on early Keeps

GARDEROBE SHOOTS :from toilets above.

WALL WALK: from which defenders could fire arrows and drop missiles.

FOREBUILDING : Protected entrance.

CHAMBER

HALL

KITCHEN

BASEMENT

CHAPEL

VESTIBULE

WELL SHAFT : Could run through several floors, or be in basement.

EXTERNAL STAIRS : If timber, could be burnt if under attack.

FIG 3.7: *A cut away view of an imaginary stone keep showing some of the features and details to look out for.*

In rectangular and the larger square-planned keeps extra strength was gained by building a partition wall across the middle of the tower. It helped to support the roof, reduced the length of floor joists, and acted as an additional barrier to attackers should they enter the building. This happened at Rochester in 1216 when the attackers blew away the corner tower and the defenders made a stand behind this cross wall. In large rectangular keeps it subdivided the spaces into separate rooms but in square-planned towers it caused an obstruction within the middle of rooms like the hall, so a series of arches and columns or even a single span, as at

FIG 3.8: CASTLE RISING, NORFOLK: *A 12th century ringwork castle containing a massive rectangular keep. The corner towers and slim buttresses on the visible side are typical of the period while the entrance doorway on the bottom right is the forebuilding which leads up to the vestibule (see fig 9.9) and then the hall (see fig 9.2). The lavish decoration on the forebuilding (see fig 3.16) and the fact that the outer ringwork bank was originally much lower imply that this was built more for show than to withstand sustained attacks.*

Hedingham Castle, could remove the problem. Keeps were often equipped with the latest features like fireplaces (only in selected rooms early on), garderobes (toilets set within the walls), a well, sometimes with its shaft running up through the wall, and even guttering. It is worth noting that many if not most stone buildings in the Middle Ages were rendered or at least painted white (hence the White Tower in the Tower of London) and the rough stone finish we often see today was never designed to be viewed.

Guttering would help protect the exterior from staining with rainwater.

CIRCULAR AND POLYGONAL KEEPS

In the later 12th century a number of experiments were made with the form of the keep. A tower with a circular or polygonal plan would in theory reduce the impact and deflect the force of a missile launched against its wall. It would avoid corners which were not only vulnerable to undermining but also required expensive quoins.

FIG 3.9: CLIFFORD'S TOWER, YORK: *A view looking down from the battlements of this 13th century keep with the top of a gargoyle that was used to channel rainwater away from what were probably whitewashed exterior walls.*

FIG 3.10: ORFORD CASTLE, SUFFOLK: *A polygonal keep (with circular rooms within) built by Henry II from around 1165-70, as part of a scheme that included a new town, church and an improved port at this coastal site. The main body of the castle is flanked by three large turrets (two of which are in the photograph) and an entrance lobby lower down to the left of the building.*

FIG 3.11

Although accommodation was limited by having round spaces for the hall and chamber, large square buttress towers built on the side of a keep provided additional space for other rooms. Despite their apparent military advantage, however, the square or rectangular keep was far more common.

Fig 3.11: EXEMPLER CASTLE: *Back in Exemplar Village, the local lord has lavished a fortune on rebuilding the previous timber and earth motte and bailey castle in stone. The mound was cleared and slightly lowered in height to fit a shell keep. The timber palisade that surrounded the bailey below is now a stone wall with a new gateway and two towers.*

The river over which the castle stands guard was essential for transporting the materials for all the building, which included the new church and the bridge.

The village itself has been replanned as a speculative venture by the lord of the manor, with a return expected from the weekly market and rents paid for the strips of land upon which the tenants have erected their single storey longhouses (see Chapter 10). Despite the disruptions of the mid 12th century these are generally prosperous times with a growing population. The village has expanded along the road on the other side of the river, due to its increasing importance as a trading post and the castle's role as a local government centre.

STILL OUT THERE

FIG 3.12: KENILWORTH CASTLE, WARWICKSHIRE: *This large Norman keep was erected in the late 12th century on top of the original motte, so that where its basement level would have been is an earth mound with an angled stone plinth covering it. As with many strongholds it was rendered unusable after the 17th century Civil War, in this case by destroying the wall to the left in this photograph.*

FIG 3.13: BOWES CASTLE, COUNTY DURHAM: *This face of the keep which dates from the 1170s and 80s shows the composition of its walls with an outer and inner skin of masonry blocks covering a rubble core, exposed at the top right. The stonework along the ground in front of it is the remains of the forebuilding which enclosed a staircase leading up to the arched entrance just to the right of centre on the first floor (see also Fig 10.13). Bowes was built by Henry II within an old Roman fort mainly as protection against raiding Scots.*

FIG 3.14: BOWES CASTLE, COUNTY DURHAM: *This interior view shows the foundations of the cross-wall in the foreground heading to the left with a gap for the doorway, the first part of its arch still projecting from the right hand wall. In the background on the first floor, which would have contained the hall, are mural chambers and on the far left the arched entrance shown from the outside in fig 3.13.*

FIG 3.15: SHERBORNE OLD CASTLE, DORSET: *There were only a few places on a castle where windows openings would be risked, usually high up illuminating a hall, chamber or chapel. In the 12th century they had round arches, sometimes two side by side with a column dividing them, and some, as in this example, had zig-zag decorations around the outside.*

FIG 3.16: CASTLE RISING, NORFOLK: *On more palatial or lordly residences decoration designed to impress rather than serve any military purpose can be found. In these two photographs there are examples of 12th century details like the overlapping arches upon a solid wall (known as blind arcading) and the columns set into the internal and external corners of the building.*

CHAPTER 4

The Baronial Wars and the Early Plantagenet Kings 1216–1307

FIG 4.1: BEESTON CASTLE, CHESHIRE: *This imposing hilltop fortification was erected by the Earl of Chester from 1225 as part of a line of castles across the middle of the country. The round face of the towers on the right command the defensive ditch while the other sides stood above sheer cliffs. This corner of the hill was further protected by an outer wall with open backed towers so if attackers overran it they would not receive shelter from crossbowmen firing from the inner defensive line. The Earl's other castles show how no single type or style of castle was exclusive to a particular period. Chartley near Stafford was a reworked motte and bailey while Bolingbroke in Lincolnshire was an enclosure type with an almost symmetrical ring of walls and towers surrounded by a wide moat, similar to Edward's famous Welsh castles but built 50 years earlier.*

A Brief History

The succession of Henry III to the throne after the death of his father, King John, in 1216 was not a straightforward matter, especially as the monarch was only nine. The crown was still in dispute as rebel barons had invited Prince Louis from across the Channel to replace him. Louis's French army, though, had been held up in sieges at Lincoln, Windsor and notably Dover Castle, and his inability to take these undermined his power and authority as a leader. When news was received of John's death, it was to young Henry's banner that many barons now directed their support. The French prince and remaining rebels were defeated by the regent, William Marshal, in 1217. Henry III who declared himself of age ten years later may have expected to rule with absolute power.

The barons were still powerful though; they had three times as many castles as the King, and he was too financially and militarily weak to rule without support from them. The King had no intention of sharing power and the two sides were inevitably drawn into battle, the barons ironically being led by Simon de Montfort, himself a Frenchman who had benefited from Henry's generosity. The Baronial Wars first went the way of the rebels with the capture of Henry and his son Edward at Lewes in 1264, only for divisions in their ranks to occur and the escape of the young Prince to lead to de Montfort's demise at Evesham in the following year. Edward succeeded his father in 1272 and was a far more authoritative ruler. He attempted to restrain the power of individuals and reform the law, without aggravating the barons, by gaining consent for his actions through regular Parliaments. Their support was important in raising taxes for his military campaigns.

The Welsh had been kept at bay since the Conquest by a line of earldoms along the border. These independent 'Marcher lords' invariably ended up vying with each other for power. While the Baronial Wars caused disarray, Llywelyn ap Gruffudd created a Principality of Wales, a strong independent state which Edward, angered by the Welsh leader's non appearance at his coronation, sought to destroy. Edward's first invasion left Llywelyn with just Anglesey and Snowdonia. Resentment at his treatment by the English, and concern about the castles that they were starting to build, inspired hopes of liberation, only for the Welsh leader to be killed in an early skirmish. His Principality was annexed to the English crown in 1283.

In Scotland in 1296, Edward's claim for the crown was successful at first and gained the submission of the Scottish lords, only for the army he left behind to be beaten by William Wallace. Although Edward regained the initiative, it was while he was on the way back to crush another rebellion in 1307 that he died.

The Castle in this Period

Battles in the 13th century were still won by cavalry, and the castle where they were based played a crucial role. It was to the castle that the losers went for refuge, remaining a danger until their surrender. For instance after the death of Simon de Montfort at Evesham in 1265, his supporters held his castle at Kenilworth for nine months, the longest siege in medieval England, surrendering merely when disease broke out and only two days' food supply remained. Castles could also make or break a king. Events might have taken a different course if Prince Louis had been able to smash through the defences of Dover Castle in 1216 and prove his qualities as a leader.

FIG 4.2: KENILWORTH CASTLE, WARWICKSHIRE: *This massive ruined castle (probably the finest and largest in England) was expanded by King John in the early 13th century (see the original keep in fig 3.12). He built the low outer wall with buttresses nearest in the photograph, then erected a dam and flooded the entire foreground of this photograph with an immense lake. Henry III then granted it to his brother-in-law, Simon de Montfort, in 1253, who promptly showed his gratitude by leading his fellow barons in revolt against the King! Kenilworth was laid siege to for nine months at the end of this Baronial War, proving impregnable and only surrendering on agreeable terms.*

Developments in weaponry were to have a marked effect on the castle in the 13th century. Prince Louis had brought over from France a new siege machine, the trebuchet, which could throw missiles with a force so far unmatched. Designers of castles now needed to look at ways of forcing the machines to stand out of range of the inner walls. Another important weapon was the crossbow. Although the English had always preferred the quick firing and more accurate bow, they now realised its potential in siege warfare where it could help to compel attackers to keep their distance.

In order to keep attackers at bay, the castle had to enlarge its boundaries, which involved even more expensive building work and longer walls that required more bowmen to patrol. It was inevitable that more castles became redundant. Henry III, for instance, reduced the number of royal castles from 60 to 47, although he still carried out work on the remaining ones. Edward continued some of his father's plans, like the extensive defensive system

FIG 4.3: GOODRICH CASTLE, HEREFORD AND WORCESTER: *A Welsh border castle that was upgraded in the late 13th and early 14th century with many of the latest military features. The 12th century square keep stands to the left and is surrounded by the later round tower and wall; the length in the middle of this view has a bend in it due to the original keep being on a different alignment to the later work.*

around the Tower of London, but towards the end of his reign it is recorded that castles such as Lincoln, Oxford and Guildford became dilapidated with plots for crops and houses encroaching on their defences.

As part of his campaign in Wales, Edward I built new castles and strengthened existing ones along the border region. His great legacy, unfortunately outside the remit of a book about English castles, was those he erected in the heart of Wales. However, it is fair to say that many of the ideas used appear in earlier English castles or were certainly present on the Continent.

Castle Types

Stone keeps continued to be built in the 13th century. For most of the castles it was their outer walls that now received attention.

▣ ENCLOSURE CASTLES

To combat the threat from improved weaponry, owners might erect a new stone wall of greater circumference around their castle. When they built from scratch the ring of towers and walls were considered so powerful that a keep or stronghold was deemed not necessary. The larger tower or gatehouse provided secure accommodation

FIG 4.4: CLIFFORD'S TOWER, YORK: *Named after the Cliffords who were the hereditary Constables of York Castle, it is a rare example of a new keep built in the 13th century when most castles were concentrating on their outer defences. It consists of four contemporary round lobes with a square forebuilding over the entrance, and originally had a roof and two floors within, the top containing the King's private apartments and the bottom a guardroom and offices for clerks.*

FIG 4.5: FRAMLINGHAM CASTLE, SUFFOLK: *Dating from the late 12th century, Framlingham is one of the earliest castles to be built with a curtain wall, open backed towers and no keep. The hall, chapel, and other interior buildings stood up against the inside face of the wall, very much as the later structures pictured here do today. A castle like this, though, is only as strong as its defenders and with the longer length of wall to cover, the seven crossbowmen who were present when it was under siege in 1216 were too few to man the twelve towers and the castle surrendered after only two days.*

and, freed from the limited space within the great towers of the previous century, the area now enclosed enabled the king and his barons to erect more impressive halls, chapels, private chambers and service rooms. Some of these were freestanding, but most were built up against the inside face of the outer wall.

The outer walls usually consisted of a short length of thick, straight, wall between towers that were greater in height. The effect of the short walls between tall towers has been compared to a curtain hanging, and they are hence known as curtain walls. The principle was that bowmen along the battlements on top of the wall and towers, and others from arrow loops in the walls, could rain down fire upon approaching attackers. With the power of the crossbow, this could force even the armoured cavalry back to a safe distance. If the attackers managed to scale the walls then the extra height of the towers meant that the bowmen on top could continue firing on the enemy as they stood upon the wall walk. Early curtain walls had square, open backed towers roughly in line with the lengths of wall

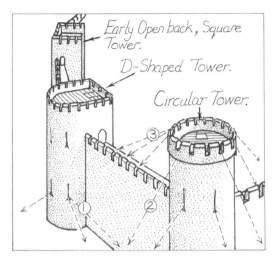

FIG 4.6: *A diagram showing three types of tower along a curtain wall. The earliest examples tend to be square in plan with open backs, while most 13th century examples are circular or D-shaped. The different levels of firing position and protruding towers gave defenders good coverage of all areas outside the walls. Attackers at the base could be shot (1), as could those further away (2), while any attackers who managed to get on top of the walls could be fired upon from the towers (3).*

FIG 4.7: BEESTON CASTLE, CHESHIRE: *A distinctive type of gatehouse from the 13th century which had two D-shaped towers, with their rounded side facing outwards, either side of a narrow gateway. Note the cross-shaped arrow slits (loops) and the pointed gateway, a form which had replaced the round arch in the 13th century.*

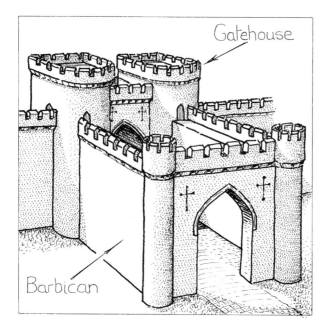

FIG 4.8: *A drawing of a simple barbican which consists of two walls projecting from either side of a gatehouse with a further gateway at the end. Not only did attackers have to fight through an extra set of gates, perhaps with a portcullis and from the end of the 13th century a drawbridge, but they would then be enclosed between the two flanking walls and made easy targets as their movements were restricted.*

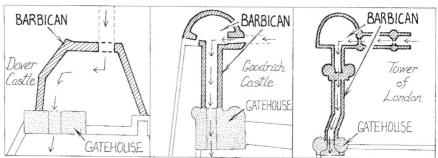

FIG 4.9: *Three different plans of barbicans showing how they could vary greatly from simple enclosed areas to causeways lined with towers, gates, and strategically placed bends.*

between them (see fig 4.5). Over the coming decades towers were built to a circular or D-shaped plan (with the rounded side facing outwards) so that they could deflect missiles from throwing machines.

With defence concentrated upon the outer wall, the castle's perpetual weak point, the entrance, received particular attention. The most characteristic gateway of the 13th century was two large circular towers with a straight wall containing the gate between them. These large gatehouses could not only hold bowmen on top or in shooting galleries within but also contained private rooms for the custodian or owner of the castle. More conventional, square-planned gatehouses were still built and both types featured a dropping portcullis, murder holes and, by the late 13th century, a drawbridge.

◈ BARBICANS

The barbican was a feature built to protect the vulnerable gateway. It had been used on earlier castles but it became universally popular in the 13th century. They conformed to no set design, their shape, size and layout depending far more on the site, space and route of approach to the castle. The idea was to trap the attackers approaching the gateway in a long, narrow passage so that defending bowmen could send arrows and bolts down upon them from the two side walls. The limited mobility within the barbican, and the kinks that were often incorporated, made getting a battering ram to the main gate a difficult task. Barbicans can range from two parallel walls running straight out from a gateway with an arch at the end, up to a longer series of walls with turns, towers and gateways.

◈ CONCENTRIC WALLS

Concentric walls were a development which tried to achieve a similar effect as the barbican. By building a second barrier beyond the main curtain wall any attackers who scaled the first line of defence were liable to be massacred by bowmen as they had little mobility trapped between the two walls. In addition, the new outer wall was built lower so that bowmen from the inner wall could more easily fire upon the enemy. Thus, with bowmen on both inner and

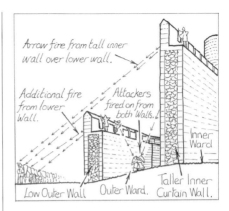

FIG 4.10: *A diagram showing concentric defences and how defenders could rain fire down upon attackers from both the higher inner wall and lower outer wall at the same time.*

outer walls, the attackers had to deal with arrow fire from all directions.

Building a curtain wall in stone was beyond the means of many castle owners; building a second, even longer one outside that, could only be afforded by the King and his mightiest subjects. Hence it is likely to be found only around great fortresses like Dover Castle (which was the first to receive concentric defences, in the 1180s) and the Tower of London.

◈ WATER DEFENCES

Castles had always had ditches or moats surrounding them. Many were just dry, perhaps fitted with pointed stakes at a time of warfare, while others which were wet may have contained only enough water to make the going tricky or just deep enough to drown an assailant. In the 13th century, as castle owners strived to keep siege machinery at a distance, more substantial water defences were dug, with in some cases lakes flooding the area

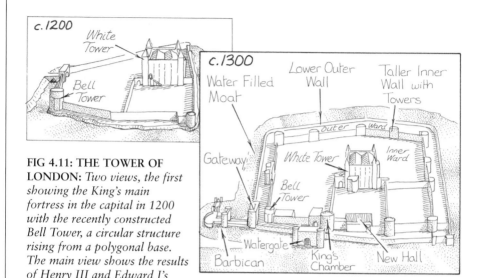

FIG 4.11: THE TOWER OF LONDON: *Two views, the first showing the King's main fortress in the capital in 1200 with the recently constructed Bell Tower, a circular structure rising from a polygonal base. The main view shows the results of Henry III and Edward I's work with their concentric defensive walls, round and D-shaped towers, water-filled moat and a new gateway and barbican. The bank of the Thames is today in line with the very bottom of the picture so that a cobbled road runs in front of the water gate, and the moat is dry.*

surrounding the curtain walls (see fig 4.2). Another advantage of water-filled moats was that they made mining virtually impossible as any tunnel would be flooded before masonry was reached. Where water defences were constructed a defended causeway and a drawbridge usually followed.

While the castle's role is still as a defended home for its lord and a base for his mounted knights, expensive revisions and enlargements are justifiable; and, although its position as a courthouse and prison has been further reinforced in the 13th century, the feudal society it was built to control is on more shaky ground. Already the lord pays the king rather than sending men in arms when called in to battle and the increased accommodation has allowed him to house his own private army.

FIG 4.12: EXEMPLAR CASTLE: *In these still prosperous times the owner of Exemplar Castle has benefited from the successful development of what is now a small market town, and with its income and that from his other estates has enlarged his principal residence. The bailey has been expanded down to the river with round corner towers marking the new extension, while the water has been directed around the castle in a re-cut ditch. The extra space within the walls has allowed the owner to build himself a large stone hall and private chambers, connected by covered walkways to a kitchen and the old hall, which is now used for storage and accommodation. The entrance has been strengthened with a new gatehouse and barbican while the old town ditch which surrounded the settlement in the previous visits has been replaced by a stone wall.*

FIG 4.12

STILL OUT THERE

FIG 4.13: YORK CASTLE, YORKSHIRE: *A circular corner tower that remains from the 13th century curtain wall around York Castle. The battlemented top has gone but one of the original low placed arrow slits can be seen to the left side of the tower so bowmen could fire at attackers along the base of the wall.*

FIG 4.14: BARNARD CASTLE, COUNTY DURHAM: *This castle which was progressively developed from the late 11th to the 14th century stands dramatically on cliffs above the River Tees. The notable feature from this period is the round tower, in the background to the left, which was built in the early 13th century.*

FIG 4.15: BROUGH CASTLE, CUMBRIA: *A window with a pointed arch, a form that was popular throughout the 13th and 14th centuries. This example has remains of reticulated tracery within it, which was common in the early to mid 1300s when the hall in which it is set was built.*

FIG 4.16: SHERBORNE OLD CASTLE, DORSET: *The remains of the north gate tower and barbican which protected the entrance on the north side of this bishop's castle (see fig 2.8). The fields above the ruined walls were the site of a lake in the 12th century which surrounded the castle hill. The thicker walls in the foreground are of the gatehouse (thicker foundations as it was a taller building).*

CHAPTER 5

The Later Plantagenet Kings 1307–1399

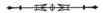

FIG 5.1: BODIAM CASTLE, EAST SUSSEX:
Built after 1385 when a licence to crenellate was received from the King, this courtyard castle was set on a new site lower down the hill than its predecessor next to the River Rother which fed the artificial lake surrounding it. Under this façade though is an impressive residence for a noble who had made his fortune in the French Wars, and as its only real military threat came from bands of raiders, it lacks the thick walls and strong outer defences of earlier castles.

A Brief History

Edward II continued the campaign against the Scots, leading the army of Edward I across the border. Unfortunately, he was no warrior, and promptly turned round and headed back to London to enjoy himself, leaving Scotland for Robert the Bruce's taking. The monarch failed to impress his subjects with military might and failed also to give the earls and barons what they really liked – victory, looting and women. When Edward II finally dragged himself away from self indulgence in 1314 he ended up leading the English army into catastrophic defeat at Bannockburn, near Stirling.

The Scots under Robert the Bruce were outnumbered three to one by the English, yet they managed to immobilise the English cavalry, by crippling the horses with spiked iron balls in the ground, and repelling their charges with long spiked lances held by tightly-packed groups of foot soldiers. From now on, archers and foot soldiers would take precedence in battle; the age of warfare dominated by the mounted knight was drawing to a close. Edward now found himself in the hands of his magnates with a country

FIG 5.2: BERKELEY CASTLE, GLOUCESTERSHIRE: *This is where Edward II met his death, and remarkably it is still in the hands of the direct descendants of the Fitzhardings who were his jailers. This same family had in the 12th century converted the motte and bailey castle by trimming the mound and erecting a stone shell keep around and above it (the higher part to the left). They then surrounded the bailey with a stone wall (the lower part to the middle and right), the inner ward that was created being filled with buildings which today date from the 14th and 15th century.*

ravaged by the worst famine in European history. In 1327, he was murdered at Berkeley Castle after abdicating in the face of an invasion led by his own Queen!

Edward III, in contrast, was a strong leader and soldier. He proved himself by defeating the Scots at Halidon Hill (near Berwick) in 1333 by combining the firepower of the longbow with the skill of the dismounted soldier. These men-at-arms were now professionals tied to the King or his lords by cash payments or retained by contracts, rather than by feudal duty. Their new military tactics relegated the mounted knight to more of a symbolic than battle-winning figure. It is during Edward III's reign that the familiar image was formed of the Chivalrous Knight and the Order of the Garter; and the tournament took on its familiar form, centred around jousting (see Chapter 10). Not only did Edward keep his magnates occupied with these diversions, but he also led them to victory against the traditional foe, France.

The Castle in the 14th century

Despite this being the age associated with the popular images of the medieval castle and knight, it was actually a time of decline in which many castles were neglected and some even abandoned. The demise of what were hugely expensive structures was due in part to the breakdown of feudalism (which was accelerated by the Black Death), the diminishing use of mounted knights after Bannockburn and a less rebellious aristocracy. Gunpowder, which is often thought to have brought about their end, was then a new discovery and is unlikely to have influenced any noble's decision to abandon a castle.

Of those castles that survived many were in the hands of the king and the great lords who adapted them for social rather than military purposes. Throughout the medieval period the king and his barons travelled from estate to estate, taking their household with them on huge wagon trains. Now, however, the lord and his entourage were more likely to stay in one place for several months. His staff were paid in cash and clothes and they were retainers, tied to their lord by contract. This 'bastard feudalism' applied also to the soldiers who formed a lord's private army who, along with the increasing number of senior staff, household servants and aspiring young nobles, required accommodation within the castle. New buildings were usually erected for this purpose within the outer bailey or ward, while the senior retainers were provided with rooms in towers or gatehouses.

The owner was also under pressure to build impressively in order to maintain the outward sign of wealth, his retainers might well desert him if they felt he was in financial difficulty. To emphasise their wealth nobles erected larger and more ostentatious halls with kitchens and private chambers attached. Their fortifications became the setting for a grand lifestyle of entertaining, music, dance and tournaments and are often referred to as 'Show Castles' or 'Castles of Chivalry'.

There still remained areas, though, where defence was important and the castle still had a role to play. After the Scottish army was defeated at Halidon Hill, the main threat from across the border came in the form of raiding. The great northern families like the Percys and Nevilles continued to build castles in the 14th century, either by adding extra fortifications to existing ones, upgrading manor houses or building from scratch. After the French regained the initiative in the 1360s the south coast of England was threatened by raiding parties and a

KEEP

STAIRCASE AND ENTRANCE

FOREBUILDING

KITCHEN

HALL

KITCHEN CT YARD

BUTTERY

SERVERY

'STRONG TOWER'

BASEMENT STORAGE

FIG 5.3: KENILWORTH CASTLE, WARWICKSHIRE: *The photograph above shows the remains of the buildings which John O'Gaunt added to the castle of the de Montforts, and the drawing to the right gives a cut away view of how they may have looked in c1400. The original Norman keep (see fig 3.12) is in the left background, in front of this is the new kitchen and service block which adjoined the vast hall with its imposing windows and a basement below for storage.*

FIG 5.4: MIDDLEHAM CASTLE, NORTH YORKSHIRE: *This keep and bailey castle was inherited by the Neville family in 1270 and they set about improving its defences, firstly by replacing its timber palisade with a stone curtain wall in around 1300, and then increasing this in height in order to fit larger and more luxurious accommodation around the inside of the wall. All of this went around the huge 12th century keep, which still stands in the centre (the higher parts in the middle of the picture).*

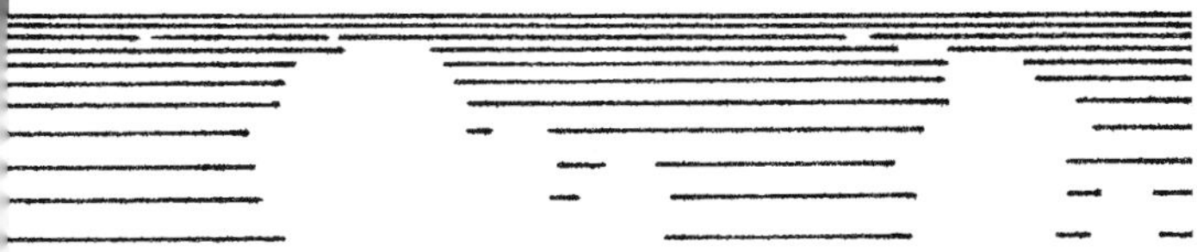

FIG 5.5: BOLTON CASTLE, NORTH YORKSHIRE: *A massive fortified manor house built on a quadrangular plan with five-storey towers in each corner dating from the 1380s. It is based around a central courtyard which is accessed through an insignificant opening on the opposite side to reduce the chance of surprise attack. The cut away drawing shows how it was also self contained, having the stables, guardrooms and even a mill on the ground floor with the hall and apartments of various sizes depending on importance arranged around the upper floors.*

CHAPEL
KITCHEN
STABLES
GATE
COURT YARD
APARTMENTS
SERVICE ROOMS

FIG 5.6: OLD WARDOUR CASTLE, WILTSHIRE: *A wider variety of styles is characteristic of later castle keeps like this example based on an hexagonal plan with a central courtyard (see fig 5.7). This was firstly a magnificent home with the only military threat likely to come from discontented peasants rather than any army. Hence there are two grand windows above the entrance marking the hall, which never would have been tolerated in earlier keeps (most of the other windows are of a later date). Although the structure now stands within an 18th century landscape park, it was originally surrounded by a walled enclosure with accommodation, stables and workshops most likely within.*

potential invasion, so money was spent on existing castles, and towns received defensive stone walls. There was also a new breed of lesser gentry who had grown rich from looting in the French Wars and who now wanted to erect impressive new homes. Many aspired to a castle; some were granted them, others built them when they had received a licence to crenellate from the King, who was especially keen for them to do so in these troubled southern counties. Fear of a rebellious peasantry also encouraged fortification over a wider part of the country and even affected bishops and monks who built new gatehouses and walls around their palaces and abbeys. The new castles that they erected took a number of forms.

▨ COURTYARD/QUADRANGULAR CASTLES

A regular shaped castle ward enclosed within a curtain wall with corner towers as used in some of Edward I's Welsh castles was a popular blueprint. With stone buildings around the inner face of the wall, the open central square was more of a courtyard than a ward. As castles now needed to provide defence against French or Scottish raiders rather than a whole army, the fortifications became more lightweight and the walls lower, with less attention paid to defensive qualities and more to magnificence and comfort. Many that were built on new sites were positioned on more convenient low ground rather than commanding hilltops where the steep ascent and limited water supply now seemed unnecessarily arduous. In the valley it was easier to keep water in the moats that surrounded these castles.

The gatehouse was in many cases still the dominant feature of the outer walls with well-defended, imposing structures making an impressive entry into the courtyard and providing accommodation on its upper floors. Fourteenth century structures tend to be rectangular or square in plan, sometimes with a round tower on each corner and an inner and outer portcullis making some, in effect, a keep-gatehouse.

❖ THE RETURN OF THE GREAT TOWER OR KEEP

In the 14th century, as castle owners sought to impress their guests and staff,

the keep with its imposing form found favour again. Another reason for building them was that now that the lord had to provide lodgings for his private army, there was always the risk that the mercenary soldiers would turn on their master should there be a problem like unpaid wages. The keep provided him with security from within as much as without!

The interiors were more lavish than in earlier keeps with larger window openings fitted with tracery patterns flooding light over the principal rooms on the upper floors. It tends to be the external detailing, though, that helps date one of these later keeps. Fashionable Continental features like machicolations, cylindrical towers, double fighting platforms and bartizans, that some owners may have seen while at war in France were fitted to keeps. Water-filled moats, drawbridges and a series of portcullises along the entrance passage were also popular at this time. These features were also found on some of the gatehouses and towers of 14th and 15th century courtyard castles.

❖ PELE TOWERS AND TOWER HOUSES

On the northern borders, the threat from Scottish raids encouraged those further down the aristocratic ladder to erect their

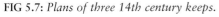

FIG 5.7: *Plans of three 14th century keeps.*

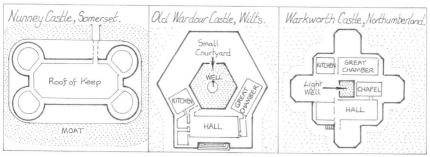

FIG 5.8: NUNNEY CASTLE, SOMERSET: *Continental influences especially from France affected the style and shape of 14th century castles, as this example from the 1370s demonstrates (although its owner John de la Mare never went there). The ring of projecting brackets around the tops of the round towers called machicolations (see fig 5.12 and fig 6.3) and the thinner cylinders which stand above these and gave defenders a second ring of fire were both fashionable details. Although Nunney resembles a courtyard castle which has been squashed so that the corner towers almost touch, it is in fact a keep (see fig 5.7)*

own towers, smaller in scale and mainly domestic, but still resembling a castle keep. From the 14th to the 18th century there were many different types built, from simple two-storey structures that acted as a retreat within a farmstead, up to imposing towers with four or more floors for a manorial lord. Some of these larger ones are still known as castles although they were never designed for counter attacking, while many are marked on maps today as pele towers.

Early fortifications along the Borders started as enclosures with timber or reinforced clay and turf walls, with the defended area known as a 'pele' (from *pilum*, Latin for a stake or palisade). During the 14th and 15th century, rectangular-planned towers were erected within them, some in timber but the finest in stone. Some, like early castle keeps, had their entrance up a ladder or steps on the first floor with access to the basement only possible from a trapdoor within, others had a separate entrance to allow livestock to be housed in the basement. The first

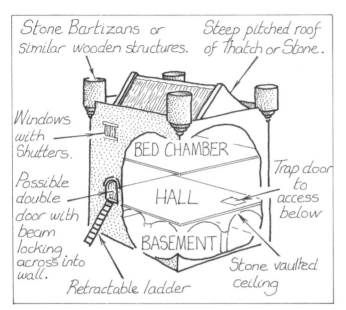

Stone Bartizans or similar wooden structures.

Steep pitched roof of thatch or stone.

Windows with shutters.

Possible double door with beam locking across into wall.

Retractable ladder

BED CHAMBER

HALL

BASEMENT

Trap door to access below

Stone vaulted ceiling

FIG 5.9: *A diagram showing what a 14th/15th century pele or tower house may have looked like.*

floor would have been a hall and service rooms with bedrooms above, while the thatched or stone roof was protected by a raised wall, sometimes with bartizans overhanging the corners.

◼ FORTIFIED MANOR HOUSES

Although some fortified manor houses are known as castles, they are not castles in the true sense of the word. Nevertheless it is worth mentioning that across England from the time of the Conquest, but particularly after the mid 12th century, lesser nobles were erecting defences around their residential halls and service buildings. By the 13th and 14th century, some of these featured stone walls and towers but they were probably only strong enough to keep out small raiding parties, and may have been more for show.

FIG 5.11: EXEMPLAR CASTLE: *The Black Death some fifty years earlier and*

subsequent outbreaks have resulted in the abandonment of numerous houses in the town, many of which have been taken over by neighbours expanding their properties. The Lord of the Manor has also been busy rebuilding many of the structures within the castle walls to accommodate his increasing household, personal army and the demands of its judicial role. This includes a taller hall, new bedchambers and service rooms, and extra accommodation for his retainers. The reverse side of this concern with magnificent building is a neglect of the castle's defences especially the shell keep, where a collapse of the motte and bridge has not been repaired and the timber buildings within are in a state of ruin.

The castle has dominated the town for nearly 350 years, but the changing ambitions and demands of the Lord of the Manor and the relative peace and security of the greater part of England are to play their part in its final chapter.

FIG 5.10: STOKESAY CASTLE, SHROPSHIRE: *Probably the best preserved medieval fortified manor house in the country, this was built for Lawrence of Ludlow, a wealthy wool merchant, in the late 13th century. He received a licence to crenellate in 1291, in this case to build the South Tower in the left background of the picture. Despite this more formidable feature the property is still a house and not a castle, its partial fortifications more for show than any serious defence. The timber-framed projection around the top of the nearest building resembles the wooden hoarding which was built upon castle walls and towers at a time of attack (see Chapter 8).*

Exemplar Castle c.1400

FIG 5.11

STILL OUT THERE

FIG 5.12: NUNNEY CASTLE, SOMERSET: *A close up of one of the towers in fig 5.8, with the projecting brackets that originally would have supported further masonry with holes in between through which defenders could drop missiles and fluids onto attackers below (machicolations). The thinner part of the tower above enabled a second line of defenders to rain arrows down over the heads of their colleagues. Both of these are unlikely to have ever been used and were designed more for show.*

FIG 5.13: MIDDLEHAM CASTLE, NORTH YORKSHIRE: *A section of the 14th century curtain wall with the gatehouse at the far end, built sometime before 1410. Note the pointed arch doorway and the diagonally positioned buttresses which would have originally supported turrets. The zig-zag feature along the top are stone brackets (corbels) which held up the battlements above and could have formed machicolations.*

FIG 5.14: OLD WARDOUR CASTLE, WILTSHIRE: *The massive windows which showered light onto the hall have a characteristic elongated, tall profile typical of the Perpendicular style of architecture, which although principally relevant to church architecture still influenced the shape of features in the halls and chapels of 14th and 15th century English castles.*

FIG 5.15: KENILWORTH CASTLE, WARWICKSHIRE: *A close up of the hall showing the imposing tall windows. Note the stone ledge around the bottom of the recesses which indicates window seats, a popular 14th century detail. The windows would have originally held heraldic glass with colourful displays of coats of arms.*

CHAPTER 6

The Wars of the Roses and the Tudor Age 1400-1603

FIG 6.1: KIRBY MUXLOE CASTLE, LEICESTERSHIRE:
This was one of the last castles built in England, by Lord Hastings during the 1480s although his untimely execution meant it was never completed. As with many 14th century castles it had a quadrangular layout with a surrounding moat, but typically of the 15th century it was made of locally produced brick. Although the gateway in the foreground features round gunports, this was really a fortified manor with too many windows and lightly made walls to resist a determined attack.

A Brief History

Henry IV spent most of his reign fighting to retain the throne he had seized from Richard II, so it was his son who benefited from the secure foundation he established. Just a decade after his father's death, Henry V launched an invasion of France, was victorious at Agincourt in 1415, entered Paris as Regent and heir to the French Crown in 1420, only to die of dysentery two years later. It was his son Henry VI, barely a year old, who became King of France. Inspired by Joan of Arc, the French revoked this title in 1435 and over the following years the English were effectively removed from France, thus ending the Hundred Years War. Henry was no warrior.

During his reign, dynastic struggles between the two rival families took place: the descendants of John O'Gaunt, the Duke of Lancaster (Lancastrians) and those of Edmund, Duke of York (Yorkists). The Wars of the Roses (1455 – 1485) only came to an end when the Yorkist Richard III was defeated by Henry Tudor at the Battle of Bosworth.

The Castle in this Period

The Wars of the Roses were fought in open pitched battles with little need for the castle and most nobles felt secure enough to dispense with their expensive fortifications. They erected only lightweight battlemented walls and water-filled moats around their expanding manor house

FIG 6.2: BADDESLEY CLINTON, WARWICKSHIRE: *Although clearly not a castle, this typical manor house dating from the 15th and 16th century still features a moat, and out of the picture a battlemented gatehouse with gunports!*

FIG 6.3: TATTERSHALL CASTLE, LINCOLNSHIRE: *This impressive brick keep was one of the additions made by Lord Cromwell in the 1430s and 40s to an existing stone castle. It was more of a palace, with increasingly grand rooms as you ascended it, rather than a military stronghold. Some argue though that it was built to protect the lord from his own personal army should they rebel as much as from any threat of invasion. Light coloured stone around the windows, running around in horizontal bands and forming the machicolation openings at the top are typical features on brick castles. The rough projection of brickwork on the lower part of the right-hand tower is from where the curtain wall ran, while the line of holes to its right was part of the corridor which linked the tower to a separate hall. The rectangular foundations in the foreground are the remains of the kitchens positioned outside the curtain wall to reduce the risk of fire spreading.*

courtyards and new palaces. Now they paid more attention to embellishing the buildings within.

One group who now found itself under threat was the clergy, whose unpopularity had made them a target for rioters. Stone outer walls, moats and strong gatehouses can still be found around bishops' palaces, abbeys and monasteries from this period.

◆ BRICK CASTLES

There were still, however, a few who decided to build new castles or at least radically change their existing ones in this period and the latest fashionable material to use was brick. Although brickwork can

FIG 6.4: HERSTMONCEUX CASTLE, EAST SUSSEX: *This brick castle from the first half of the 15th century features fashionable machicolations and a double fighting platform on the two towers flanking the gateway, yet it was principally a Grand House rather than a strong fortification.*

sometimes be found in Norman structures, the bricks were reused Roman ones from ruined buildings. From the 14th century the art of brickmaking was reintroduced from the Low Countries, and in selected pockets along the east and south-east of the country, those wealthy enough could invite a brickmaker to bake, either on site or close by, a set number of bricks for their house or castle. At this stage the bricks were irregular, often appearing long and thin (those at Kirby Muxloe Castle in fig 6.1 were 9½×2⅓ inches compared with approx 8½×2¾ inches on more recent machine made bricks). The pattern formed in the wall by the way the bricks were laid (bonding) was most commonly one layer of bricks lengthways followed by one on top with the end facing out (English Bond), although due to the irregular sizes this could often go out of synch! Some castles had stone mouldings for windows and doorways, with horizontal strips around the structure, while others had diamond patterns (known as diaper patterns, see Fig 6.1) made out of dark blue/grey bricks

that had been overburnt or affected by wood smoke during firing.

FIG 6.5: EXEMPLAR CASTLE: *The castle that has dominated the small town since the late 11th century has now been abandoned by its owner, who has built for himself a fine new mansion on the other side of the river, away from the noise and smells of the busy market place. The fact that the castle has survived this long is due to its continuing role as a local court and prison, although the parts not used in the judicial process have fallen into ruin or have been encroached upon by neighbouring properties. The castle has been largely ignored in the current growth and rebuilding of the town, and with most now renting their land and properties from a lord who lives elsewhere, it no longer plays a central part in their daily lives.*

This fictional fortification like many actual town castles only fulfilled its true role for some three to four hundred years. Yet today in towns and villages across the country they still stand, if only in part.

FIG 6.5

STILL OUT THERE

FIG 6.6: KENILWORTH CASTLE, WARWICKSHIRE: *As with many castles that continued to be used as homes in the more peaceful 16th century, large new windows were inserted. Typically the upper three here are square headed rather than arched, and are divided by vertical (mullions) and horizontal (transoms) bars.*

FIG 6.7: KIRBY MUXLOE CASTLE, LEICESTERSHIRE: *A late 15th century stone window frame set with a fashionable square top.*

FIG 6.9: OLD WARDOUR CASTLE, WILTSHIRE: *A Classical doorway dating from the 1570s which replaced the previous pointed arch opening, to make a grander entrance to the great hall. Any Renaissance influence like this is likely to date from the 1550s until the late 18th century.*

FIG 6.8: FRAMLINGHAM CASTLE, SUFFOLK: *A typical 15th or 16th century gateway with a flat, wide archway set within a square head, in this case with the owner's coat of arms above it, which had replaced an earlier opening in this 12th century castle.*

FIG 6.10: KIRBY MUXLOE CASTLE, LEICESTERSHIRE: *A 15th century round gunport designed to take small, possibly hand held firearms. They are typically found on gatehouses as a threat to those crossing the bridge rather than being a crucial part of the castle's defences.*

CHAPTER 7

The Changing Fortunes of the Castle

FIG 7.1: MORETON CORBET CASTLE, SHROPSHIRE: *The 13th century castle to the left of the picture (see fig 9.12) was modernised by Robert Corbet with this shockingly modern style building in the foreground added to it. Robert died in 1583 before the whole project was finished, and the house was then burnt down by troops in the Civil War leaving these dramatically contrasting ruins side by side.*

The Demise of the Castle

The reason for the demise of the castle is often blamed upon the advent of gunpowder. It is worth noting, though, that cannons in the 14th and 15th centuries were cumbersome, little better than earlier throwing machines, and were more likely to be found within the castle firing out. During this period in France, Spain and Italy castles continued to be built, with them being adapted to cope with the threat of gunpowder. The English aristocracy therefore could have rebuilt their fortifications to withstand cannon fire had they wished but medieval castles were

FIG 7.2: POWIS CASTLE, POWYS: *Some owners never had the funds, especially Catholic families who were deprived of the financial benefits of office during the 17th and 18th centuries, to replace their ancestral castle with a Classical mansion. The large windows, and 17th century steps cannot disguise the battlemented round towers of the original medieval castle. The courtyard in the foreground was originally a bailey with its curtain wall built into the later buildings behind the trees on the left.*

immensely expensive and domestically inconvenient, so were more likely to be left to deteriorate. The only exception were those on the Northern Borders which had to wait until more settled times in the 17th or even the 18th century.

Another influence was the breakdown of the feudal system, which once had the castle at its centre. The cavalry forces based in castles that had stood at the forefront of the medieval kings' feudal army, now played a lesser role in an army composed of foot soldiers and archers, fighting in open pitched warfare rather than besieging fortifications. The

expectations and ambitions of the very men who had built these castles were changing. Now they were learning the Humanities, with languages, art, dance, music and the classics as important as military education. No longer were they judged purely upon the size of their private army: now the Tudor gentleman displayed his wealth by means of ingeniously designed houses featuring symmetrical façades, courtyards and the latest in Renaissance adornment. Castles therefore did not disappear just because of changing warfare, they were neglected because those who had to maintain them

FIG 7.3: BRIDGNORTH CASTLE, SHROPSHIRE: *The 12th century keep of this castle was blown up by Parliamentary troops in 1646, but this half remained, standing at an angle three times greater than that of the Leaning Tower of Pisa! Note the V shape at the top, which shows that its original roof ran down into a central gulley, and the line of holes, which mark an original timber floor.*

saw them as archaic and irrelevant. Their only acceptable features were the battlements, towers and turrets – for the power and authority they implied rather than the military advantage they gave - and these continued to be used on colleges, houses and churches.

Although this general trend saw the country house replace the castle as a lord's home, a number of them were retained. Some were strategically important garrisons like Dover or Carlisle, others had been so lavished with domestic apartments that they had become palaces rather than fortifications, as at Windsor and Kenilworth. Many of those in cities and county towns survived as courtrooms and prisons, their lordly owners building themselves new houses in private parks away from the busy centres. A few families, through either choice or lack of funds, continued to occupy and adapt their ancestral homes.

During the Tudor period there grew a proud awareness of England as an island and nation rather than as part of a medieval family empire. Accordingly, defence was now thought of on a national scale with counties and towns, rather than just individual lords, paying towards its maintenance. The most notable example of this are the coastal forts, like the one at Deal in Kent, which are often referred to as castles, but were actually the latest in artillery installations. As they did not provide accommodation for their royal builders, they were not true castles.

The Civil War

Despite the neglect of medieval castles many were to have one final military role during the English Civil War of the 1640s. Ruined fortifications were patched up and their wards and baileys echoed again with the sounds of soldiers preparing for battle. Warfare had changed, though, since they were last manned. In Oxford, for instance, which was the Royalist headquarters, the castle as a whole played the part of a keep, being a last-ditch stronghold, while the city itself was the bailey with the zig-zag style ditches around its perimeter acting as its curtain wall. Other castles and some country houses were re-fortified by individuals and proved an irritation to victorious Parliamentarians who had to lay siege to them when trying to winkle out the last Royalist supporters. Once hostilities were over, some 50 to 60 castles were rendered unusable, with their fortifications, especially strong points like the keep, blown up (slighted) by Cromwell's troops. To the common folk the destruction of this symbol of the Norman feudal order was a popular move and castles continued to be a target for demolition and pilfering even after the monarchy had been restored in 1660.

The Revival

By the late 18th century the way in which enlightened men perceived the world was

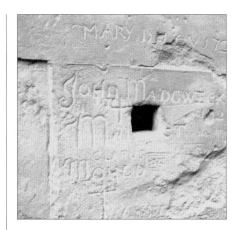

FIG 7.4: OLD WARDOUR CASTLE, WILTSHIRE: *In the 17th and 18th centuries when castles often lay in ruin and were treated with disrespect, they became targets for looting building material and graffiti artists. Many castles today still have examples of visitors' names and dates carved into their masonry.*

changing. The obsession with the Classical Order and the rules of symmetry and proportion that had dominated architecture for over 200 years started to wane as individuals began to appreciate the Picturesque. This movement, inspired by paintings of scenes from nature, freed architects from their strict restraints and allowed them to experiment with shapes and styles. This was also a period when British aristocrats, burgeoning with wealth from trade and industry, searched for a home-grown national identity rather than one from Greece or Rome, and they found it in the medieval world of the Magna Carta and the Chivalrous Knight. Others who had risen from humble backgrounds through trade and industry to positions of power or fortune used

FIG 7.5: LOWTHER CASTLE, CUMBRIA: *Although it has an outline which resembles a castle, the symmetrical façade with a central block and wings either side, large windows at low levels, and the fact that it all dates from one period identify this as a mock fortification. This mansion was built for the Earl of Lonsdale (as in the Lonsdale Boxing Belt) by Robert Smirke from 1806-11, but has been left as a shell since partial demolition in 1957.*

images of these past times to give the impression that their family had ancient lineage. These factors, along with the patriotic fever that arose at the time with the threat from Napoleon across the Channel, inspired many aristocrats from the 1790s to erect their new country houses in the forms of medieval castles.

These magnificent buildings, such as Belvoir and Eastnor Castles, were ingenious works of modern architecture, but as they were houses that used battlements and towers for their rousing associations rather than any military reality, they are not true castles. They differ visually from their medieval predecessors by using masses of large windows, especially at low levels; being built in one go with their masonry the same all over; having symmetrical façades; and lacking military features like moats, ditches, outer walls and arrow or gun ports. Unlike true castles which were usually in towns, standing upon a rocky outcrop or on a well-defended riverside position, the 18th and 19th century versions were erected in parks, away from the noise and smell of the city.

It is also worth noting that the remains of many genuine medieval castles can be

FIG 7.6: ARUNDEL CASTLE, WEST SUSSEX: *A number of castles that survived the 17th and 18th centuries as family homes were restored or rebuilt in the medieval revival of the 19th century. In many cases the Victorians' domestic demands, the architect's flare, and the fact it was being changed into a mansion drown out the original structure, as is the case here with the mass of windows! You are in fact visiting a 19th century mansion - and in this instance a very dramatic one at that - which also thankfully retained its 12th century shell keep relatively intact (see fig 3.4).*

found within parks, often near a later country house. As the castle was the seat of the local lord he simply built his new manor house next to the old structure, perhaps reusing its masonry. Later the village that was associated with the castle was removed by the lord to create a new park, thus changing the landscape in which it had originally stood.

In the 19th century a reaction against industrialisation inspired the Victorian obsession with medievalism. It became fashionable to rebuild existing castles in a romantic style. The grey stone and oak panelled interiors of many castles that are still inhabited today are the work of Victorians and lack the vibrant colours and whitewashed walls of the original rooms. New castles continued to be built in this new Gothic period with asymmetrically arranged towers and façades making them appear, at first glance, to be more 'authentic'. Even in the early 20th century one of our great modern day architects, Edwin Lutyens, used the form of the medieval castle as inspiration for the house he built at Castle Drogo in Devon.

SECTION
II

THE CASTLE
IN
DETAIL

CHAPTER 8

Defensive Features

FIG 8.1: *An imaginary view of an attack upon a besieged castle to illustrate the different devices that could be used.*

The above view illustrates some of the methods and siege engines used by attackers upon a medieval castle. The rules of medieval warfare usually meant that the castle's owner or his constable were notified of an intended attack, and thus had time to prepare for the impending siege. This could involve gathering missiles, making arrows and bolts, cutting down trees and flattening houses surrounding the castle walls. Farmland was scorched and ponds and wells poisoned to deprive attackers of supplies while timber hoarding (A) was built around the top of towers and shutters (B) were fitted in the battlements. Most important, though, was to stock up the cellars with food like cheese, pickled meats and biscuits made from grain that could last the long months of a siege, as these and the castle well would be the only source of food and water.

The attackers would have various methods of breaking through into the castle depending on their own resources, the reputation of their leader and the type of defences encountered. They could erect mobile towers covered in hides (C) called belfries ('belfry' originally meant siege tower and was only later applied to church bell towers) and use their lowering bridge at the top to get over the battlements. Others might use scaling ladders (D) which were made in a variety of types with hooks at the top to grip the masonry, although defenders could use poles to push them off. Mobile wooden shelters would protect miners (E) chipping away at the mortar in order to bring part of a wall down, or a battering ram (F) hammering against the gateway or a section of masonry, the latter often known as a cat, sow or musculus (mouse) from the way it appeared to pick or gnaw away at the castle.

A time-consuming but effective way of bringing down a tower or wall was to dig under it. A team of miners (many experienced from lead mines in Germany) would tunnel towards and then under a vulnerable corner (G), support the masonry with posts and then light a fire around them, burning the wooden supports and collapsing the tower above. Walls could also be smashed by a variety of throwing machines; two notable types were the mangonel (H) which catapulted a projectile, and the trebuchet (I), probably first used in England in 1216, which slung a missile by means of a counterweight at the other end of the arm. If the garrison did not surrender the castle at the first flexing of the attackers' muscle (as often happened), then a counter or siege castle (J) would be erected to protect the attackers from sorties by the besieged soldiers.

The castle builders had to bear these

forms of attack in mind when erecting a castle and the fortifications that survive today represent their solutions to these problems.

▩ MOATS, DITCHES AND RAMPARTS

The first obstacle an attacker was likely to tackle would be outer rings of earthworks encircling the main fortification. The quickest and most effective way of protecting one's home has always been to dig a ditch and pile up the spoil on the inner side to make a rampart. At the time of the Iron Age hillforts this had developed into impressive and sometimes complicated systems of ditches and banks, especially around the perpetually weak entrance. The earliest castles built in this country still relied on these simple and easily built features as the first line of defence. Dry ditches might be lined with stone slabs or clay and then filled with lines of pointed stakes bound together in open scissor shapes called herrisons (from the French word for hedgehog). On valley bottom sites where there would usually be a spring, stream or river the ditch was flooded, preferably to a depth greater than a man could stand. The attackers would have to try and make a causeway across by filling in the ditch with available material bound into bundles, which could even include animal carcasses.

In the late 12th century, when builders started to concentrate on strong outer walls, they also tried where possible to dig moats around them to protect the stone foundations from miners. At Kenilworth the surrounding fields were flooded to create a vast lake (see fig 4.2) which when it was besieged in 1266 not only prevented undermining but also kept the attackers' siege engines at a less effective distance.

Today grassed-over ditches and ramparts are often all that survives of the early timber and earth castles. While

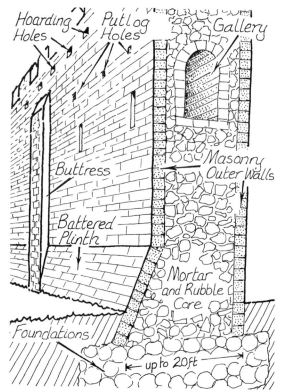

FIG 8.3: MORETON CORBET CASTLE, SHROPSHIRE: *One way to identify buildings from different periods is to look at where the sections meet. In this example the wall to the right is from the 12th century keep, while the wall to the left, which from a distance seems of the same date, simply butts up against the other wall with the horizontal lines of mortar not matching the ones on the keep. It is most likely that the left hand wall is later and was built up to the earlier keep.*

FIG 8.2: *A diagram of a curtain or castle keep wall with a section through it showing how it could have been constructed.*

looking at them, remember they were dug out and built some 900 years ago, so their height and steepness of slope will be greatly reduced. Many castles that survived to become homes often had their redundant ditches and ramparts filled in or flattened to make way for gardens.

◈ THE WALLS

The next line of defence was the outer wall. On early castles this would have been made using vertical timber posts or planks (a palisade) mounted upon an earthen rampart, although it was appreciated right from the start that these were very vulnerable to fire, even when defenders tried draping wet hides over them or soaking the wood with water.

Stone walls were typically built with outer faces of cut sandstone, limestone or granite with a thick core of rubble and mortar, though where these stones were not easily available flint and similar stones made a good substitute (the Normans loved Caen stone from their homeland, but this was very expensive to transport over).

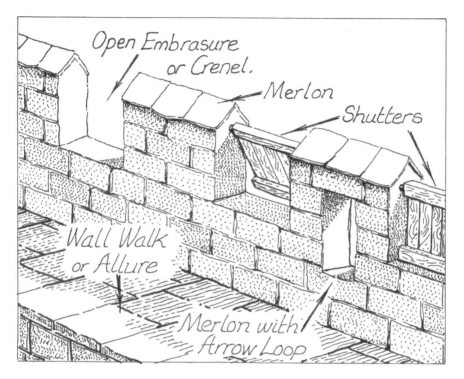

FIG 8.4: *A diagram showing the parts of the battlements.*

The base of the stone wall was vulnerable to a battering ram, so the lower section was angled outwards, making a battered plinth, which also had the advantage of sending any missile that had hit the wall above rolling back towards the attacker. Curtain and keep walls were the targets of throwing machines like the mangonel and trebuchet, so they were built very thick, 10-12 ft with a base up to 20 ft in some cases. This was usually strong enough, though any galleries running through them were weak points. Height was also important so that projectiles thrown over them would miss the vulnerable buildings erected along their inner face. While the walls were being built higher, the wooden

scaffolding used was secured to the structure with horizontal posts running into the stonework. Today where the timber or the mortar left within the wall has fallen out, you can see a putlog hole.

◼ CONCENTRIC DEFENSIVE WALLS

A second outer ring of walling: see Chapter 4 for a full explanation.

◼ BATTLEMENTS

The top of the walls were finished off with what we today refer to as battlements, a protective, tooth shaped parapet with a wall walk or allure behind it for the soldiers to stand upon. The gaps from which defenders could throw missiles are

FIG 8.5: *The view on the left is of the wall walk and battlements on top of the curtain wall at Framlingham Castle in Suffolk. The square openings along the bottom narrow down to plain vertical arrow loops on the outside, while the crenels originally had shutters fitted (some still have their grooves in the stonework to their sides) though permanent protective walls in brick have been inserted later. The right hand view is of the battlements around the top of the keep at Richmond Castle, North Yorkshire. Note the top of the roof above the hall in the bottom right.*

known as embrasures or crenels, and could have been fitted with wooden shutters which were hinged from the top so a defender could fire and let them swing shut before an attacker could respond. The raised sections between are called merlons, and were originally solid though later ones often had arrow slots (called loops) inserted in them. The crenels were usually 2-3 ft wide while the merlons between were nearly twice this width. Many of the battlements that appear as decorative trimming on later buildings are typically of equal size (these are often referred to as crenellations).

▓ HOARDING MACHICOLATIONS AND DOUBLE FIGHTING PLATFORMS

As stone castles developed it became usual at a time of impending danger for the castle's carpenters to build a timber hoard (sometimes called a brattice) over the top of vulnerable stretches of the castle's defences, in particular the towers and gatehouses. Although the base of the curtain wall was covered by fire from projecting towers, these structures themselves required protection and hoarding, overhanging their crest, enabled men to drop missiles and hot substances from holes underneath onto any attackers below. Timber beams projecting out from holes in the masonry supported the wooden walls, which were perforated with arrow loops and could be covered with wet hides in the height of battle as fire protection. Despite this risk the greatest danger came from throwing machines, as

Timber roof and walls

Arrow Loops

Holes for dropping missiles. *Sockets in Masonry.*

FIG 8.6: *A drawing of what a temporary hoard on top of a castle tower may have looked like. Some may have had extra angled supports underneath (as in fig 5.10) and a different arrangement to hold up the corners.*

a well-directed missile could easily smash the timber structure. Although hoarding does not survive today the holes left in the masonry for the supporting joists do, usually in the form of a horizontal line of square sockets around the top of a tower or length of wall (there are good examples at Rochester Castle). The timber jetty on top of the tower at Stokesay Castle in fig 5.10 gives some impression of what they may have looked like.

In the 14th and 15th centuries these temporary structures were replaced by permanent stone versions which were popular on the Continent called machico-lations. These consisted of a horizontal line of stone brackets (corbels) supporting a masonry or brick wall above with holes in between for dropping missiles etc. As at this time defence was of less concern to castle owners, machicolations may have been added for their fashionable rather than military qualities. It was also at this time that fighting platforms were built on some castles. These could be a narrower cylinder extending above the top of a round tower (see figs 5.8 and 6.4) or a separate level below the wall walk punctured with openings covered by shutters (see fig 8.7).

FIG 8.7: TATTERSHALL CASTLE, LINCOLNSHIRE: *The left hand photograph shows the top of the castle keep with three levels of firing positions possible from the towers, the upper wall walk and the arches underneath. The second photograph is from under one of the lower arches with the wooden grilles covering the machicolations through which defenders could pour hot substances or drop missiles upon attackers.*

▨ ARROW AND GUN LOOPS

In early castle warfare the bow was not an essential weapon of defence as they could do little damage to chain-mail-armoured soldiers from high up on the battlements. During the 12th century the more powerful crossbow appeared. Although it fired at a much slower rate, it could reach further and puncture armour. This had the effect of forcing the attackers, including the now vulnerable knights, back to a less damaging distance from the outer walls. There had always been narrow slits in the walls of castles which splayed out on the inside to permit the maximum amount of light in, but now purpose-made gaps in the walls, correctly called loops, were built facing out to the attackers or on the sides of towers to cover the base of the curtain walls.

Arrow loops can be found in many forms. As bows are in a vertical position when fired a single tall loop would suffice, but the crossbow – which is held horizontally – may have benefited from a cross-shaped opening (croslet). Round holes at the end of each arm or a fish tail shaped slit at the bottom gave additional coverage of fire.

By the 15th century the originally crude, ineffective but frightening gun was beginning to influence castle design, and a number of them were fitted with round gun loops, usually in the gatehouse. It is just as likely, however, that the owner was trying to impress guests with the latest in military fashion!

▨ DRAWBRIDGES

It was not until the late 13th century, almost as the castle began to decline, that one of its most familiar features became popular, the drawbridge (correctly called a *pont levis* or turning bridge). Previously

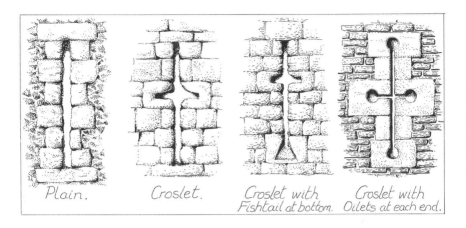

Plain.   Croslet.   Croslet with Fishtail at bottom.   Croslet with Oilets at each end.

FIG 8.8: *Four types of arrow loops, from the simple and generally earliest vertical type to more elaborate croslets.*

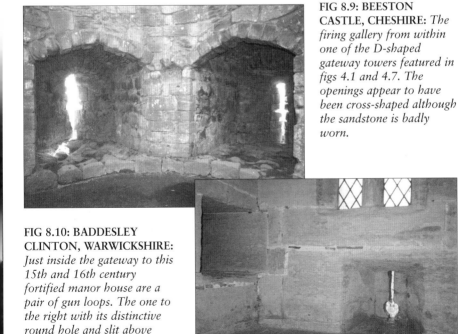

FIG 8.9: BEESTON CASTLE, CHESHIRE: *The firing gallery from within one of the D-shaped gateway towers featured in figs 4.1 and 4.7. The openings appear to have been cross-shaped although the sandstone is badly worn.*

FIG 8.10: BADDESLEY CLINTON, WARWICKSHIRE: *Just inside the gateway to this 15th and 16th century fortified manor house are a pair of gun loops. The one to the right with its distinctive round hole and slit above covers the moat, while the square opening to the left guards the bridge.*

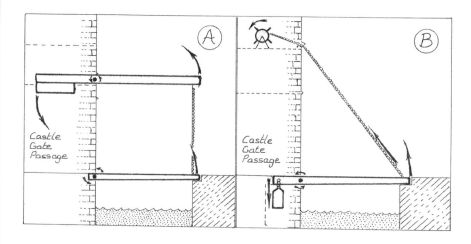

FIG 8.11: *Two types of drawbridges. They both relied on a counter weight which was almost equal to the amount required to lift the bridge, so that when the defender pulled or wound up the chain only a small force was required to tip the balance and raise the heavy wooden bridge. (A) was the earlier type and used two horizontal beams with counter weights within the castle walls, very much like a lift bridge over a canal. (B) was more common and was raised by chains wound up on a capstan with a heavy counter load, which appears to have been directly attached to a small overhang on the castle side of the hinge although there were probably variations in this design. Holes high up on the gatehouse where the chains passed through and gaps below the entrance where the bridge was hinged can today indicate where a drawbridge once stood.*

bridges across either dry or wet moats were usually fixed, so when trouble beckoned an area of planks across it might be lifted to create a hole. The earliest drawbridges had a pair of horizontal beams running into the gatehouse, very much like a lift bridge on a canal (fig 8.11A). The later, more familiar type, was hinged on the castle side while the far end was raised by chains wound up by a capstan or windlass in the tower above (fig 8.11B). The weight of the bridge would have been too much to lift on its own so counter weights could have been used, fixed to the end of the beams in the earlier version, or hanging from the castle side of the bridge in later ones. Another advantage was that when the drawbridge was raised it added another barrier between the attackers and the interior.

◼ PORTCULLISES AND GATES

The next obstacle facing attackers would be a grille called the portcullis (from the Old French *porte-coleice*, meaning sliding door). These familiar castle icons were lowered by chains from a chamber above the gateway, through a slit and grooves (which often survive today) down in front of the gate. The portcullis helped to protect the gate from fire and battering, and some could also trap attackers between it and the door so defenders could easily pick them off through arrow

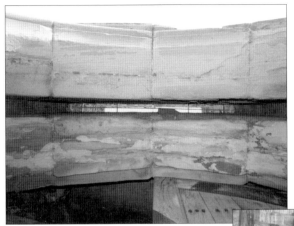

FIG 8.12: KIRBY MUXLOE CASTLE, LEICESTERSHIRE: *Looking up at the underside of the gateway arch you can see the slot through which the portcullis would have dropped. This is a common sight on most castles, and don't be surprised to find more further along the gatehouse passage.*

loops to the sides or murder holes above. The portcullis could only be removed by lifting, so defenders could wedge it in place from above to withstand attackers armed with levers. The more advanced gatehouses of later castles would often have an inner and outer portcullis, while some had a series of them through the gate passage.

The main gate or door in a medieval castle was usually a heavy timber structure made from planks fixed to a wooden grid, not dissimilar to the portcullis, with lines of iron studs helping to hold it together. A drawbar slotted horizontally across the back and into the masonry on either side to keep it shut. Although few genuine medieval gates survive, the grooves for them and the rectangular sockets for the drawbar, can still be found.

🔲 MURDER HOLES

Murder holes, or *meurtrières*, were openings in the ceiling just in front of a gate or in the passage beyond. They were so called because it was believed that they were used by defenders in the chamber above to drop hot liquids or molten lead down upon the unfortunate attacker

FIG 8.13: BOOTHAM BAR, YORK: *In this room above the gatehouse passageway on the city walls is a wooden portcullis, now fixed in place above the slot through which it would have been lowered.*

FIG 8.14: BADDESLEY CLINTON, WARWICKSHIRE: *The doors to many a medieval castle may have looked something like this example from c1500, although they would have usually had a flat outer surface rather than with the raised beams shown here.*
FIG 8.15: CASTLE RISING, NORFOLK: *In the middle of the underside of this arch, halfway up the entrance passage steps is a rectangular-shaped murder hole.*

(however, lead was so valuable it is unlikely to have been wasted in this way). It is more likely that water was poured through these holes to quench any fire that the attackers had built in order to burn down the gate. They would have also been useful for spying.

◈ POSTERN GATES AND SALLY PORTS

The day to day opening and closing of the huge gate would have driven a porter mad so a smaller door may have been fitted within it or a completely separate entrance provided. This postern gate could range from a humble doorway sited at the rear of the castle to a gatehouse with defensive features (the entrance in fig 5.1 was a postern gate).

It should also be remembered that the castle was a platform for launching attacks and when under siege a surprise sortie against the surrounding army, or missions to get supplies or assistance were essential. A sally port was the point from which the defenders could discreetly leave (the postern gate may have been used), and would often be a doorway off the ground level so it could not be battered, with a retractable ladder to take soldiers down.

CHAPTER 9

Domestic Rooms and Features

FIG 9.1: *An imaginary scene of a hall within a keep which stands on the first floor with the timber ceiling joists (A) above the line of deep splayed window openings to maximise the light (B). The double arched windows on the far wall (C) are open with shutters fitted to the sides while the three are linked by a passage called a mural gallery running between. The walls are plastered and decorated with a series of red lines simulating a masonry effect (D), while wall hangings (E) cover part of the lower wall. Cleanliness of your hands was very important in medieval times and a laver (F) of some type would have been provided near the entrance for washing them. The floor in this example is made of wood (G) with straw spread over to soak up the rubbish and spillages which land upon it. Heat and further light is provided by a freestanding brazier (H) as a fire was not possible directly on the timber floor unless a box of sand with stone slabs was placed below it. To the sides are trestle tables which could be removed when required, for instance when court proceedings were taking place. The lord sits proudly upon a raised platform called a dais (I), while behind him towers a canopy (J) which helped keep draughts out.*

Although it is the castle's defensive features that make it distinctive in our eyes, it was its role as a home that was of equal importance to the owner. Behind the battlemented walls, arrow loops and portcullises the king or baron created luxurious suites of rooms, designed as much to impress as to accommodate his family, dependants and servants. The owner would expect somewhere to eat, sleep and pray, secure locations to store food, drink and valuables, and at least one room large enough in which to hold gatherings, administer the estate and deliver justice. These domestic quarters remain today only as rectangular foundations set in the lawned interior of the ruined castle or as vanished floor levels within an empty keep. Yet even from such barren clues it is possible to identify what a room or building was used for from its size, type of decoration, the features within and its position in relation to others. This chapter will help you recognise these signs as well as describe the original role and appearance of the domestic rooms.

The Principal Rooms

▓ THE HALL

The heart of any castle was its hall. The

FIG 9.2: CASTLE RISING, NORFOLK: *Although this was actually a passage knocked through the wall of this 12th century keep at a later date to provide better access to the kitchens, it gives an idea of what a mural gallery would have looked like. (A real one would usually have been on a floor higher than this, as the arched opening and square floor joist holes on the opposite wall show this passage ran along the bottom of the hall.)*

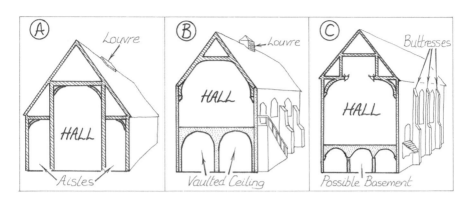

FIG 9.3: *Three types of hall that could have been found within the inner bailey of a castle. (Note the louvre openings on top to allow the smoke from the central hearth to escape if fireplaces were not provided in the side walls.)*

estate which the castle was built to protect was run from it, the lord and his household ate and slept in it, guests were entertained in it, and legal matters were settled there. Although the hall was built for the king or baron, you would have been more likely to find a constable or castellan residing there as the ever-mobile medieval monarch or noble would stay at each of his residences for only a few weeks at a time. The constable was responsible for the security of the castle in his absence, and its ability to resist an attacking army was a reflection upon his character and dedication as much as the strength of the fortifications. Another principal servant of a lord was his steward or seneschal, who was responsible for feeding the household and invariably ran the estate which supplied the raw ingredients for the lord's table (the word originally was 'sty-ward', the man responsible for the pigs).

Unfortunately this form of communal living did not suit the increasingly refined medieval lord and even in some of the earliest royal castles separate rooms were provided for him. By the 14th and 15th centuries the hall had become a splendid expression of the owner's wealth but he was more likely to be conducting his business, dining with the family and retiring to bed in his private apartments. Sometimes, the servants would be provided with a separate hall for eating and sleeping. The hall in these later castles was used for celebrations and entertaining guests while its legal role continued, in those that were retained as a courthouse and prison. At Oakham in Rutland, the medieval hall is still used as such today.

The hall within a keep would usually be on the first or second floor (see figs 3.6 and 3.7) with a basement or cellar below and would often be of two storeys in height (fig 9.1 shows how they may have looked). The higher level would usually hold larger window openings, some of which were connected by a mural gallery (a passage which ran through the wall itself), which was popular in 11th and 12th century halls. In the largest keeps the span for the roof timbers would be too great and the strength of the walls weakened by their length, so a cross or

FIG 9.4: NUNNEY CASTLE, SOMERSET: *The ruined shell of this 14th century keep has a gaping hole on this entrance side made by Oliver Cromwell's cannons in 1645, exposing the interior beyond. The hall is recognisable by the tall window openings in the middle of the hole (on the second floor in this case). Above this are slightly smaller windows with their tracery in place, marking the private chambers, while below you can make out the top of square headed openings which were probably knocked through at a later date. The large square holes would have held the major floor timbers across with the smaller joists running from left to right between them.*

dividing wall was built from one side to the other to reinforce the structure and reduce the lengths of floorboards and wooden beams. In some keeps the hall would be on one side, in others an arcade (a series of arches supported on columns) was knocked through to make one large room, while at Hedingham Castle in Essex a huge single span arch, the trickiest but most convenient solution, dominates its fine Norman hall.

In the bailey there were no such constraints and a large rectangular building was usually built. The earliest halls were aisled, with two rows of timber posts or stone columns supporting the massive span of roof above (fig 9.3A). This was restrictive on space so in later halls improved types of roof trusses in conjunction with buttresses outside held the structure together without the inconvenient posts inside. The more

FIG 9.5: *The interior of a medieval hall and different types of screens.*

modest stone hall may have been a two-storey structure with the hall on the upper floor above a vaulted basement, and the entrance up a set of steps at one end (fig 9.3B). By the late 14th and 15th centuries spectacular halls with perpendicular windows emphasising their great height and finely decorated hammerbeam roofs were the height of fashion for the few who could afford them (fig 9.3C).

The decoration within was far more colourful and luxurious than today's restored or ruined examples would suggest. The walls were whitewashed or they could have been plastered, although this was expensive early on as it had to be imported from Montmartre (hence called 'Plaster of Paris'), so it was not until gypsum was found at Purbeck in Dorset that it became more commonly used. A popular decoration was to brush red lines upon the finished surface to simulate masonry, while pictures painted directly onto the wall became common from the mid 12th century. Further colour and a degree of insulation could be provided by painted cloth or the more expensive tapestry wall hangings which had the advantage of being able to be rolled up and taken with the lord's baggage train to his next residence. Some later halls had timber panelling or wainscotting covering the lower parts of the wall.

The floor, often of timber in a keep, or stone, tile or compounded earth if in the bailey, would be strewn with rushes, leaves, straw or hay which would soak up the daily mess and in a well-kept household would be regularly replaced. Windows which were no more than slits in lower rooms could be modest arched openings on the upper level of the hall, with shutters or oiled cloth keeping the draft out. Glass began to appear in the 13th century, but as it was so expensive it was often set in portable frames so the lord could take it with him to his next residence. Large windows with tracery (the pattern made by masonry pieces within the opening) appear in the more secure late 13th and 14th century, and had permanent glass painted with heraldic symbols, although many still had shutters until a much later date.

Within the hall of a keep, there could be various positions for the entrance and seating of the lord, a general example is shown and described in fig 9.1. In the later halls sited within the inner bailey the layout usually conforms to that shown in fig 9.5. At one end was a raised platform known as the dais (A) on which sat the lord in a modest painted chair, with a canopy above (B) as much to keep the draughts out as emphasise the importance of the position. In some cases the high table could be sited within an oriel window (C) to the side, although this is usually only found in 15th century examples, to engulf the owner in light and enable him to see who was at the entrance. The roof trusses (D) and timberwork were typically painted, although where a central hearth (E) was still in use they would have been blackened by the rising smoke. (Most later stone castle halls were fitted with fireplaces.) At the opposite end from the dais would have been the screen (F) which helped to keep out draughts from the entrance behind, by forming a screens passage (H). It also gave the opportunity for a minstrels' gallery (G) above it where musicians could play. In earlier halls the screen was portable (I) but by the 14th and 15th century they were fixed, typically with two openings and elaborately carved (J). The entrances beyond led to the buttery and pantry and either through one of these or via a corridor between them one reached the kitchen.

Today when looking at a ruined or partially ruined castle the hall can be identified in several ways. Within the shell of a keep it will normally have a number

of larger windows with round or pointed arches, possibly with tracery still within them, on the first or second floor. The various floor levels can usually be recognised from horizontal lines of square holes which held the joists in place. In many keeps later square-headed windows have been knocked through to give more light, but these usually date from the 16th century. Where the halls that were built within the bailey still stand they are typically high rectangular structures with tall windows along the sides and two or three doorways at one end (see figs 5.14 and 5.15). It is often the case that they only survive to foundation level although there is a good chance that the largest rectangular shaped remains, perhaps with the footings of buttresses on their outer edges and twin rooms at one end, will be the great hall.

◫ GREAT CHAMBER

The great chamber or solar was the private room for the owner of the castle in which he could dine and sleep away from the household. As the king and his barons sought greater privacy throughout the medieval period, the role of the room increased in importance and a number of chambers or a suite of rooms were common by the time the first country houses developed in the 16th century.

The great chamber was also where the king or the baron would keep their money and jewels under the watchful eye of the chamberlain and possibly his deputy treasurer, and hence it was important that the room was in a secure location. They first appear alongside the hall in the Norman donjons at the Tower of London and Colchester Castle and then more usually above it in the keeps of the 12th and 14th centuries (see fig 9.4). In castles where the great hall was up against the wall of the inner bailey the chamber would

FIG 9.6: OLD WARDOUR CASTLE, WILTSHIRE: *The left hand photograph shows the hall today with the tell-tale double doors leading to the service rooms. The drawing to the right is how the same view may have looked when originally built, with the timber screen partitioning off the entrance passage. The thicker lines are the features that can still be seen in the photograph. The groove that runs between the doors in the photograph marks a modern roof which was inserted long after the floor and ceiling of the hall had collapsed.*

often be next to it in a tower or building.

The room may have been as lavishly decorated as the hall, with wall hangings, paintings and large windows with tracery. Heating would have probably come from freestanding braziers until fireplaces became common in these important rooms in the 13th century. The most prominent fitting within would have been the four poster bed with its surrounding curtain. This kept out the draughts and gave the occupants privacy from the members of the household who would have visited or kept guard over the room. Although there was little furniture in medieval buildings, the great chamber was likely to contain a chest, a chair and a cupboard, and possibly an aumbry (a cupboard built into the stone or brick walls). There may have also been a wash basin and a wooden bath tub made from a cask or barrel hidden behind a curtain. King John had a portable bath and his own bathmen to accompany him.

Today the great chamber can usually be identified from its close proximity to the hall, accessed from the end opposite the service room doors and often up a stairs or via a lobby or antechamber. You should expect it to have large windows and an impressive fireplace, although this might be a later fitting.

CHAPEL

Daily life in the medieval castle revolved around religion, and every castle would have had at least one chapel and a chaplain or chancellor to look after it. As clerics were the only ones who could read and write in the early medieval period,

FIG 9.7: ORFORD CASTLE, SUFFOLK: *The chapel built over the entrance to this polygonal keep (see fig 3.10) has the altar to the left (east end) and low stone seats with columns on either side and arched canopies above around the other walls. Originally the room would have been colourfully painted but must have been marred by the portcullis which originally rose up on the right hand wall. The second view is a close up with the altar on the left and an aumbry (a stone wall cupboard) for storing sacred vessels to the right above an arched opening with a small sink (a piscina) in which they were washed. These are normally found like this to the south side of the altar.*

they also took care of administration, usually assisted by clerks (when the king discussed business in the hall it was carried out behind a screen, the Latin for which is *cancelli*, from which the chancellor is named). The owner of the castle would have had a private chapel which would normally be near to the hall or his great chamber, while another location was in a forebuilding when these were added to the keep. In addition to the one in the keep, a second chapel or church is likely to be found in the bailey for other members of the household.

Reflecting its importance, the chapel was usually the most lavishly decorated of castle rooms and would have been richly painted in vivid colours. The room was roughly laid out on an east-west alignment as are all Christian churches, with the altar to the east and the entrance to the west (worth remembering when trying to identify rooms or foundations). Next to the altar there would have been a sedile or priest's chair, some form of bowl or depression for holding the holy water, a piscina for washing the sacred vessels and an aumbry for storing them. There may have also been a squint, a small horizontal shaft or hole through which the owner of the castle could keep an eye on proceedings within the chapel.

FIG 9.8: RICHMOND CASTLE, NORTH YORKSHIRE: *The wall in the foreground of the left picture contains the remains of a first floor chapel, including the horizontal groove in which the floor sat and a piscina in the arched recess. The narrow opening to the right of this looks like a squint, which would have enabled the occupant in the great chamber which stood behind this to see Mass. The right hand view is of an earlier chapel in the same castle, built in the bottom of a tower in the outer wall, with a tunnel vaulted ceiling. The altar was set under the window and seating was provided under the arched canopies on the right.*

FIG 9.9: CASTLE RISING, NORFOLK: *Although this is the entrance vestibule leading into the hall, in this restored state it gives some idea of the standard and size of accommodation the senior members of the household would have expected of a private chamber within a tower or gatehouse.*

▧ PRIVATE CHAMBERS

As the number of household officers grew and younger members of the ruling class attached themselves to great barons, the owners of castles had to provide more accommodation of a superior kind to that given to the mercenary soldiers and permanent members of the household in the bailey. Many were more humble versions of the lord's own chamber, positioned in one of the towers along the curtain wall or in the gatehouse above the

FIG 9.10: *The left hand picture shows one of the tunnel vaults in the cellar on the ground floor of the keep at Sherborne Old Castle. These date from the mid 15th century after the original timber ceiling was burnt down. When the great tower was built in the early 12th century the only way into the cellar was via a trapdoor and ladder from above, the opening at the end is a later addition. The right hand view shows a rib vaulted ceiling in the cellar which is on the ground level of the strong tower at Kenilworth Castle and dates from the late 14th century.*

entrance. Someone like the constable may have even been provided with his own lodgings, as was the case at Pickering where a complex of timber-framed buildings were erected for the man who lived there permanently in his lord's absence. In later castles a more substantial range of buildings may have been built to provide accommodation.

▨ CELLARS, BASEMENTS AND DUNGEONS

The room that stood at ground level or partially below it within the keep or under a large building like the great hall was most likely to be used as a cellar. It was here that food and drink could be stored in cool surroundings along with armaments. In a few later castles this space could be more correctly termed a basement, for instance when it was used as a servants' hall at Tattershall Castle.

Where possible the cellar or basement had a stone or brick vaulted ceiling made from arches supported upon columns, to allow fireproof storage for the food supplies that were vital in a siege, and provide a better surface for the floor of the hall above. Any openings in the wall would be no more than slits to provide air and a small amount of light, so the walls would often have been whitewashed and braziers or torches may have been employed to provide greater illumination.

It is ironic that the one room we always associate with the castle, the dungeon, is probably the one that the original builder never provided. There was simply not the demand to supply one as the medieval justice system was very much different from today. A suspected criminal would be tried by a jury consisting of local people, and hence to avoid a family feud later he would usually be found not guilty. For those found guilty, even for simply stealing an amount over 12 pence the punishment was hanging. The only circumstances where a prison was required would be the holding of the suspect awaiting trial, although this process could last a number of years for the unfortunate few! As the numbers in this situation would have been low, a secure room within the castle would have sufficed. It could be in a tower or most commonly in the cellar of the keep where, with no large window openings and limited access, there was little chance of escape. As the owners of the castle moved out of the keeps and lived in more palatial accommodation within the bailey from the 13th century, the old great towers continued to be used as prisons. This association with locking suspects up in the keep is probably where the word dungeon came from as it is derived from *donjon* (the French word for lordship) which was the earlier name for this building.

Some castles may have had more permanent prison accommodation, especially if they were occupied by the county sheriff (who was invariable the king's constable at the castle) or were within the areas governed by Forest Law. Others may have had small cells or *oubliettes*, which were no more than pits accessible only by a trapdoor, for holding suspects, who in these hidden locations were often forgotten! Later, as many castles developed into prisons, the more familiar scene of chained and manacled prisoners behind bars in damp, dark underground chambers is likely to have developed.

It is also worth noting when visiting cellars and basements that fallen rubble from the collapsed buildings and the general build up of waste over the centuries has raised the land around a keep or tower so that rooms which today are underground may have originally been on ground level.

Domestic Features

Although most luxury fittings have long since rotted or have been removed, there are a number of domestic features which were the height of luxury in their day and still survive in some castles today.

▧ Fireplaces and Chimneys

The first fireplaces appeared in castles around the turn of the 12th century with the smoke escaping out through gaps in the wall. It was not for another generation that the first proper chimneys were built, usually round or square in plan with a pointed cap on top and the smoke exiting through slots below this. These transformed the use of the hall, which was one of the few rooms to be fitted with them, clearing space in the middle where the old central hearth fire had stood. It must also have meant that the colourful painted ceilings and walls were no longer blackened by soot! It was only from the 13th century that other important rooms started to have their own fireplaces fitted.

These early fireplaces were usually a projecting hood supported by columns or corbels (brackets), which presumably helped trap the smoke as wall openings and early chimneys created little draw. Later

FIG 9.11: FRAMLINGHAM CASTLE, SUFFOLK: *The lower section of the chimney in the foreground with the thin arched opening dates from the late 12th century. The upper brick part is a later Tudor addition extending the chimney's overall height.*

FIG 9.12: MORETON CORBET, SHROPSHIRE: *A view looking from the cellar up to a ruined hooded fireplace on the first floor hall of this late 12th/early 13th century keep. The columns, capitals and projecting pieces of masonry either side of the opening supported the hood which is now gone, though at this angle you can also see the flue running up through the wall.*

ones are recessed into the wall in the conventional manner, with at first a more pointed arch and then as fashions changed in the 14th and 15th centuries a flatter one often surrounded by a decorative chimney-piece featuring coats of arms and heraldic symbols. Today, with the plaster stripped off, earlier fireplaces can be seen above or behind ones which were inserted later.

▧ STAIRS AND STAIRCASES

Spiralling and straight stone staircases were an essential element of any tower, keep or gatehouse. In early examples timber ladders or steps were used, but as

soon as these buildings were updated in stone, staircases made from segment shaped pieces of masonry were erected. The wide end was set within the surrounding curved walls while the pointed end was finished in a circle, which when positioned one above the other formed the cylindrical newel post up the middle of the spiralling staircase.

Defence was an important factor when building a staircase or inserting one at a later date. As they created a gap within the walls they made a weak point for attackers' siege engines to aim for, so in some cases they were built up the outside of the wall

FIG 9.13: *A drawing of how a simple hooded fireplace like that in fig 9.12 may have originally looked.*

FIG 9.15: BROUGH CASTLE, CUMBRIA: *An example of a small and simple fireplace inserted into a chamber above the gateway passage and possibly dating from the 15th or 16th century.*

FIG 9.14: *Two fireplaces surrounded by decorative chimneypieces. The left hand view is a 15th century example from Tattershall Castle decorated with various shields and scenes, including at each end the pear-shaped treasurer's purse of its owner, Ralph Cromwell. The right hand view is a later surround from the 16th century in the great chamber at Old Wardour Castle. Note the herringbone pattern to the bricks and tiles on the rear wall of both fireplaces.*

to retain its full strength. If the enemy managed to get within the structure then the staircases might be built in opposite corners on each level so attackers would have to fight across each floor in order to reach the chambers above. In some the staircase may have been built so that the defender coming down had his sword arm free to strike the attacker coming up, known as a turnpike arrangement -

FIG 9.16: *A drawing of a spiral staircase showing how the segmented-shaped steps were set into the wall for support as it was built up, while their round ends formed the newel column in the middle.* **FIG 9.17:** *The left hand view shows a newel staircase rising anti-clockwise. In this case a right handed attacker climbing the stairs would have room to swing his sword at a defender coming down, so it was more usual for the stairs to rise clockwise to turn the advantage the other way. The right hand view shows a straight flight at Richmond Castle keep, which would have greatly weakened this section of wall, so this may be why they rise up the side of the structure facing into the bailey, away from any attackers' siege engines.*

although this would have been a problem if he had entered over the wall at the top and was himself coming down the stairs!

⬧ GARDEROBES

One of the great appeals of a castle to children is the passages leading off to secret chambers. They might, however, run down them with less enthusiasm if they knew that they were likely to be medieval toilets! Most of the principal domestic rooms would have been provided with at least one lavatory, privy or garderobe, or as medieval men would have known them gongs, draughts or jakes. The major concerns in their design and positioning were to avoid odours drifting back into the main room, and to

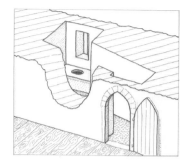

FIG 9.18: *A section cut through the wall of a keep or tower showing the two turns the passage makes from the doorway in the hall or chamber to the garderobe under the window on the outside wall, in order to reduce draughts that would bring the odour back into the room. The length of passage and number of turns will vary depending on the individual site and type of tower.*

FIG 9.19: *Two garderobe towers. The left hand view is of Middleham Castle, North Yorkshire while the right hand example from Bowes Castle, County Durham has the outer skin of masonry stripped away to show the two openings that would have held the toilet seats and the chutes leading down to the arched outlets at the base.*

remove the waste so it did not create a huge stink around the castle.

If the walls were thick enough, as was usually the case in a stone keep, then the garderobe could be built within them, usually down a short dog-legged passage which was designed to avoid a draught blowing back the odours. Doors might be fitted to the entrance of the passage and potent herbs strewn around the area to further reduce smells. If the wall was too thin then a timber or stone extension could be built out on brackets (corbels) so it hung directly above the moat or ditch, or a garderobe tower with a number of privies within could be built onto the outside to cater for larger numbers.

The toilet itself was simply a bench with a hole in the top which led down a shaft into either the moat, some form of flushing drain or a deep pit. Where they simply drop down into the surrounding moat, the bottom of the shafts were finished off in an arch or slit which directed the waste into the water. In a few cases a drain was provided through which a stream could be diverted to carry the waste away. If this was not possible then a large pit could be dug below, the smells rising from which must have been undesirable for the owner, and a nightmare for the poor man who had to clean it out. In large castles a mudator latrinarum was

FIG 9.20: *Examples of outfalls from the garderobes or latrines. The left hand set of four is at the base of Orford Castle keep, while the right hand example is from Nunney Castle.*

employed to perform this task, although he is perhaps more appropriately known as a gong fermor (farmer)!

The problems with siting the garderobe and the complaints they generated meant that by the end of the medieval period they were being replaced by close stools, which were chamber pots covered by a closed top with a hole in, which at first could be found in the great chamber and later in separate closets.

Today the garderobe can usually be identified as a narrow doorway leading out of a room, down a short passage with at least one turn and then ending on the outside wall, usually with a window opening and in some the remains of a bench seat. Below these on the outside face of the wall you can often find the base of the shafts with one or more arched openings or slits with a chamfered (grooved) back which directed the waste out into the moat (see fig 9.19 and 9.20).

▓ WELLS AND WELLSHAFTS

For a castle to survive a siege it was

FIG 9.21: ORFORD CASTLE, SUFFOLK: *This arched opening with a small basin and drain off it is actually a urinal, set in the wall of a passage in this 12th century keep.*

essential to have a good supply of drinking water. This was trickier than it would at first seem as many castles were sited upon a rocky highpoint where there was little surface water and even those in a valley had

FIG 9.22: *Two castle wells. The left hand example is within the inner ward of Beeston Castle, and as a result of its lofty position the well had to be dug 370 ft deep! This incredible task shows how important a secure water supply was. The second example is on top of the motte at Berkhamsted Castle and would have once been within the shell keep that stood here.*

their moats polluted by waste. A well was the obvious solution but even here care had to be taken to ensure that the underground water it reached was not contaminated with effluent from sewage pits!

Due to its importance the well is often built into the keep or within the outer walls of a shell keep, a bailey or an inner ward. In the case of the keep it could simply be in the ground floor of the basement or in later, more elaborate structures within the courtyard in the middle. Others had a well dug beneath the wall or corner tower with a shaft extending up through one or more levels, with doorways on each floor to access it. If there was no keep in the castle, a main or additional well can also be found in the bailey, often sited near the kitchen for use in cooking and cleaning. Where they stood in an open area they may have had some form of decorative cover that also held the winding mechanism and bucket. Many were stone lined for the top half of their drop, which strengthened the shaft and may have helped protect against contamination.

FIG 9.23: BODIAM CASTLE, EAST SUSSEX: *A well situated in the base of one of the castle's circular corner towers which is still in water.*

99

CHAPTER 10

Service Buildings and Estate Features

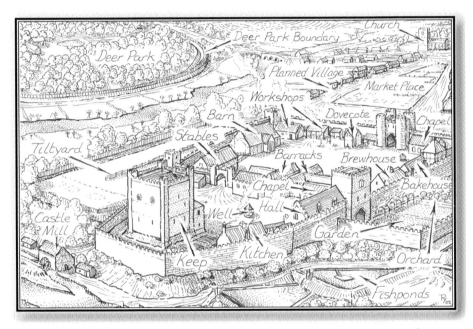

FIG 10.1: *A view over an imaginary medieval castle and its immediate surroundings.*

The king or baron's lifestyle of fighting, hunting and feasting had to be supported by numerous servants producing and maintaining the weapons, game, food and drink. In medieval England, though, there were no village shops from which to purchase supplies and although the ever mobile household would bring a certain number of staff and goods with them, the majority had to be brought in from the local estate. Bearing in mind that it might have to withstand a siege sometime in its life it was important that the castle was self sufficient.

The majority of rooms and buildings that stood within the castle boundary were there to accommodate staff and soldiers, for the preparation and storage of food and drink and for the production of goods related to the smooth running of the household. As the domestic facilities started to take precedence over the

FIG 10.2: *An example of what a late medieval or Tudor kitchen may have looked like. The fire (A) held within metal firedogs cooks the food supported on cob irons (B) and the spit (C) which is rotated by the wheel (D) and probably turned by a young kitchen hand. The fat is caught in a dripping tray (E), while other food is heated in pots hanging from the rail (F), with spare spits hung above the fire (G). Other features include the oven (H) and the central table (M). The stove (I) used for gentle cooking had fuel stored in the recess (J), air gaps (K) to help the charcoal burn, and cooking pots suspended above on either trivets or a crane (L).*

military side, a wider variety of specialised rooms and buildings were erected on a larger and more permanent scale than had been necessary in early timber castles. The remains of many of these today still bear distinctive features or are in a position that helps to identify their original use. This chapter explains the roles of these rooms and buildings, and highlights some of the details by which they can be recognised.

▣ KITCHEN

If the hall was the centre of the castle and estate, then the kitchen was the focal point of the service buildings. Although the Victorians idealised the Middle Ages as a time of chivalry, the kings, barons and knights of the period were far more concerned with filling their stomachs, there being no better way to impress their guests than providing them with an immense feast and banquet. Gluttony was the order of the day and a huge kitchen was an essential part of any castle.

The medieval kitchen would have been dominated by huge arched fireplaces or open ranges within which a hearth would

FIG 10.3: STANTON HARCOURT MANOR, OXFORDSHIRE: *One of the few remaining medieval kitchens in the country. The conical top has just below its bottom edge a dark gap, currently windowed but originally it held louvre openings which could be controlled by boys running up a spiral staircase from the kitchen on the ground floor to vary the ventilation.*

roar away cooking meat suspended upon a spit above. The immense heat given off was such that the men would appear to be stoking a furnace rather than cooking. These fires were the main consideration in deciding where to site the kitchen as they had an irritating habit of burning down the whole structure within which they were housed. For this reason the kitchen was usually a separate building connected by a passage or pentise (a covered walkway) to the hall, or if sited within the keep it would often be on the ground floor

with a stone vaulted ceiling above to reduce the fire risk. Distancing the kitchen from the diners also had the advantage of keeping the noises and odours away, although during the long procession by which food was brought along the passage, through the hall and up to the lord's table everything was likely to go cold! It is also worth noting that in this period a lot of the cooking was done outside on open fires, although as with barbecuing today this must have been weather dependent.

Baking ovens, which were dome shaped apertures with small arched doors, were built to the side of fireplaces or within a wall with brick or stone linings. In order to bake, the interior was filled with fuel and left to burn with the door shut until the correct temperature was achieved (they could tell this by the colour of the flame). Then the ashes were swept out and the oven resealed with the bread or pastry within. Some foods required a more delicate heat source and chaffing dishes suspended above charcoals or earthenware pots placed in the burning embers provided this. In larger kitchens permanent stoves may have been built, which were raised stone benches with holes upon the top in which metal grilles holding the charcoal sat, with apertures below for cleaning.

There would have been little furniture other than wooden tables for the preparation of food and sinks carved out of stone for washing. A well, somewhere in the floor of the kitchen or close by outside, provided water for cooking. Another feature that can occasionally be found is a waste chute, accessed through a small doorway and running down through the wall to a pit or the moat below. The kitchen floor of stone, tiles or beaten earth would have been covered with straw or rushes which would help soak up the waste, while there might be

FIG 10.4: MIDDLEHAM CASTLE, NORTH YORKSHIRE: *The kitchen here occupies the ground floor of the 12th century keep, with a huge pointed arch fireplace to the left (it was originally open through to the room behind) and a set of wells in the floor to the right.* **FIG 10.5: BERKHAMSTED CASTLE, HERTFORDSHIRE:** *A 14th century kitchen with the curved brick back of an oven to the left and the rectangular opening of a fireplace on the right.*

shallow channels in its surface which drained out through holes in the bottom of the wall. The walls themselves would have been whitewashed and later ones perhaps plastered. In earlier castle kitchens the fire may have been open against a wall or in the middle, so at the top of the open rafters of the ceiling there would have been some type of louvre opening to let the smoke out.

Today the kitchen is one of the more easily identified rooms or buildings. It will be near to the great hall, and is usually accessed through or between the service rooms at the opposite end of the hall from the dais. Look for the huge fireplaces, or at least their bases, and ovens with their distinctive curved, usually brick-lined backs. Find a well within a square or rectangular foundation near to the great hall and there is a fair chance that this area was the kitchen, while drain holes from the sinks or floor gulleys found near the base of the outside wall are another guide.

FIG 10.6: MIDDLEHAM CASTLE, NORTH YORKSHIRE: *A distinctive small, arched opening to a baking oven.*

FIG 10.7: OLD WARDOUR CASTLE, WILTSHIRE: *A pair of aumbries, wall cupboards which would have had doors across, in this case in a service room off the hall.*

It is worth noting that there was often more than one kitchen and separate rooms may have also been provided for baking or cooking meat.

🔲 BUTTERY AND PANTRY

It was usual in the medieval castle to have a buttery and a pantry side by side at the low end of the great hall (opposite the lord's table on the dais which was also known as the high end). These were accessed through two doorways (see figs 9.5 and 9.6) although in some a third entrance stood between them which led down a passage to the kitchen.

Most of the time these rooms can only be identified by their position at the end of the hall, though as they held items that were valuable like wine and spices an aumbry (wall cupboard) might still be found in the stone or brickwork.

🔲 BREWHOUSE

In the medieval period water was not considered safe to drink. As a result, ale was drunk at mealtimes as the brewing process would remove any impurities.

There may have been a brewhouse within the castle or the outer bailey where a variety of strengths of ale were produced including stronger tipples for special occasions. There would have been a large copper in which the liquids were heated and a vat in which the mash (mixing of malt with water) took place (the round base of this may survive today). Later, in the 15th century, soldiers returning from the French Wars created a demand for beer, that is ale flavoured with hops, which became popular with the upper classes, even being consumed at breakfast.

🔲 FARM BUILDINGS, WORKSHOPS AND BARRACKS

Although today the castle bailey may look bare, when originally built it would have been a thriving work place echoing to the sounds of hammering metal, sawing wood and screeching animals! There were two storey stables with the horse pens below and hay storage and accommodation for grooms above. There would be dovecotes housing pigeons, which provided meat and eggs for the table and were also used for communication. Alongside these would have been the carpenters' workshops and blacksmiths' forges.

In early castles the feudal lord expected his knights and peasant soldiers to live elsewhere, with knights providing their own horses and armour. From the 14th century, great lords built up their own private armies and had to provide permanent accommodation for their mercenary soldiers; these timber or stone barracks would have stood within the outer bailey.

🔲 TILTYARDS AND TOURNAMENTS

The tiltyard was an area of relatively flat land near to the castle on which tournaments could be held. The tournament developed in France before the 12th

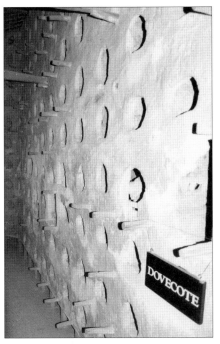

FIG 10.8: TATTERSHALL CASTLE, LINCOLNSHIRE: *Although not a medieval dovecote but a plaster insertion made into a room within a corner tower sometime around 1700, it gives an impression of what their interiors would have looked like (although they would normally have had square holes formed by gaps in the brick or stonework).*

FIG 10.9: KENILWORTH CASTLE, WARWICKSHIRE: *The rather grand Tudor stableblock with a timber frame above the sandstone base. The large doorway in the foreground is a later insertion.*

FIG 10.10: RICHMOND CASTLE, NORTH YORKSHIRE: *This enclosed area called the Cockpit on the side of the triangular-shaped castle was the site of a medieval garden, although now laid out in a modern style. The photograph is taken from the great chamber where a doorway led onto a wooden balcony where the owner could admire the lawns below.*

century, as a training exercise for cavalry soldiers, and the nature of these early events is aptly described by its name at the time, 'a mêlée'! It had crossed the Channel by the time of Henry I, although his grandson Henry II banned it, only for it to be restarted in 1194 when it was realised that the French might be better soldiers because of their training.

It is not easy to clearly identify an area as a tiltyard, although documentary evidence may help to recognise them at individual castles. For instance it is known that Edward III redeveloped Windsor Castle specifically as a backdrop for the tournament while the causeway that currently links the car park to the main gate at Kenilworth Castle was used as one.

GARDENS AND ORCHARDS

The medieval castle was not just grand buildings surrounded by noisy workshops and muddy yards. It is likely that either within or just outside the walls an enclosed, quiet area was set aside for a garden, often overlooked by the owner's private chambers. These were unlikely to contain decorative planting schemes, but rather had rough grass lawns, perhaps for early sports to be played on, paths under arbours through which ladies could promenade, some raised flowerbeds and even ponds and fountains. There were also kitchen gardens in which the herbs and flowers used for medicine, cooking and perfume were grown and an orchard of fruit trees would not be far away.

▨ DEER PARKS

One type of designed landscape that was likely to be laid out near to a castle was a deer park. These were enclosed, roughly circular areas, up to a mile or more across, in which the owner farmed deer, the venison from which was reserved for special ceremonies or guests. They were surrounded by an outer bank with a wooden fence upon it and a ditch on the inside to prevent the deer escaping. This boundary is known as a park pale and may be found as such today on Ordnance Survey maps. Within the park there would be a keeper's cottage, sometimes a lodge for the owner, and a pond or stream as a water supply for the animals. Although some existed before 1066, it was the Normans who began establishing them on a large scale so that by 1300 there were more than 3,000 parks across the country.

As their popularity declined many were reclaimed as farmland or simply became known as Park Wood, while others may have been adapted into garden schemes. In some locations you can still find the faint banks and ditches that surrounded them.

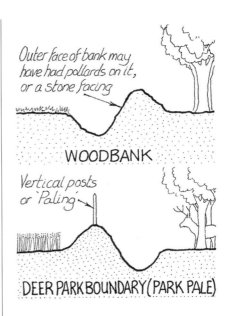

FIG 10.11: *A diagram of a deer park boundary (park pale) compared with a bank which often surrounded medieval woods, where the ditch is on the opposite side to keep animals out of the wood rather than deer within it.*

▨ FISHPONDS

Keeping a supply of food throughout the season was a constant problem for the owner of a castle. Dovecotes and deer parks were just two of a number of sources; another, which was especially important through the meat-free period of Lent, was the fishpond. Virtually any pond was suitable for farming course fish as long as there was a flow of water available that could be controlled by sluices. They were usually dug in groups so the fish could be put into compartments depending on size. Although they are more common around abbeys and manor houses, most castle owners away from the coast must have had access to this source of food in the days before sea fish could be transported inland.

▨ MILLS

Another source of revenue for the owner of a castle was the toll he charged for grinding corn at his mill. These were usually powered by a water wheel as the windmill did not become widespread until the castle was declining (the tower in fig 3.2 had the castle mill positioned directly below it). Another type of mill found within some castles is one where the horizontal, round grinding stone is turned by a horse or other animal, presumably to supply flour for the castle's own consumption.

FIG 10.12: MIDDLEHAM CASTLE, NORTH YORKSHIRE: *To the right are the circular remains of a horse mill, while the feature to the left is the base of a huge oven.*

FIG 10.13: BOWES CASTLE, COUNTY DURHAM: *A photograph showing the common situation of parish church next to the castle. (The stone foundations in the foreground are the remains of the entrance to the forebuilding, see fig 3.13.)*

CHURCHES

A building that is nearly always found standing near to the castle is the parish church. Saxon lords often established them next to their halls as a status symbol and a source of income. The Norman castles that were erected on or near these Saxon halls would have retained the church site although the building seen today would have been rebuilt since. There are a number of deserted castle sites where the church can be found on the edge or even within the grassy banks and ditches of the old bailey defences.

On new sites a church may have been built for the populace of the town or village, sometimes positioned strategically so its tower could be used as a defensive look out, perhaps at the other end of a ridge or hill. In the Northern Border regions there are still a number of church towers that acted as miniature keeps for the endangered clergy.

FIG 10.14: CASTLETHORPE, BUCKINGHAMSHIRE: *The earthworks are all that remains of this 12th century castle with a motte and two baileys, as is often the case, leaving the medieval church with which it was originally associated standing on its own.*

▓ PLANNED VILLAGES AND TOWNS

A final, often overlooked feature of the land surrounding a castle is the town or village in which they are usually set. You should expect to find that the layout of these settlements was in some way shaped by the castle owner in the medieval period and the pattern that they created is often still discernible. What today may appear a rustic, haphazard village may have once been as regular as Milton Keynes!

The earliest castles were built within existing county towns, where areas were often ruthlessly cleared of houses before the defences were dug around them. Although the outer ditches may have gone, the circular pattern of buildings that bordered it or were later erected on top of it may remain. In some cases the castle was constructed upon a ridge, above an existing settlement perhaps down by a river. The owner later laid out a new development along the hill, which despite the tricky access up to it and the problem with a water supply, became the centre of the town that grew up around its market. Today, the earlier settlement seems like a suburb: Windsor and Bridgnorth are two examples.

It was common particularly in the 12th and early 13th century to establish a market adjacent to a castle so the owner could make money from the tolls charged and possibly from rents for the prime house sites bordering the market place. Some were successful and developed into towns, others stayed as no more than a village, while some failed and remain as just impressions in the grass. Today these rectangular or triangular open spaces bordered by houses may survive as village greens, car parks, or occasionally still markets and are frequently found on the approach to castles. In other well-established towns the market space may have been built upon at a later date, but its outline should still be visible on a map.

FIG 10.15: CASTLETON, DERBYSHIRE: *This Peak District tourist spot below Peveril Castle (fig 3.1) may today appear a rustic, randomly developed village. It was in fact a planned settlement laid out in the late 12th century as a commercial enterprise to attract traders and craftsmen. Note the straight lines of buildings forming a grid.*

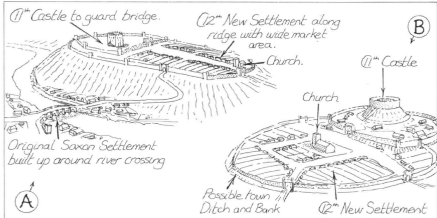

FIG 10.16: *Two views of imaginary planned settlements. In (A) a castle was erected overlooking an important river crossing and then in the 12th century a town was laid out along the castle ridge. In many situations like this today, expansion of the last 200 years has seen buildings spread up the slopes, making the two original elements of the town appear as parts of one large mass. In (B) a square or grid plan could be laid out around a central market place. Later break up of property boundaries and encroachment onto the green can disguise the original regular layout in many apparently randomly developed villages.*

SECTION
III

QUICK
REFERENCE
GUIDE

TIME CHART

Note: Dates can only be approximate as castles will have features from many different periods. The castle symbols that are shaded indicate that this is the date when the keep was built; clear ones denote the time when the majority of the existing buildings were raised.

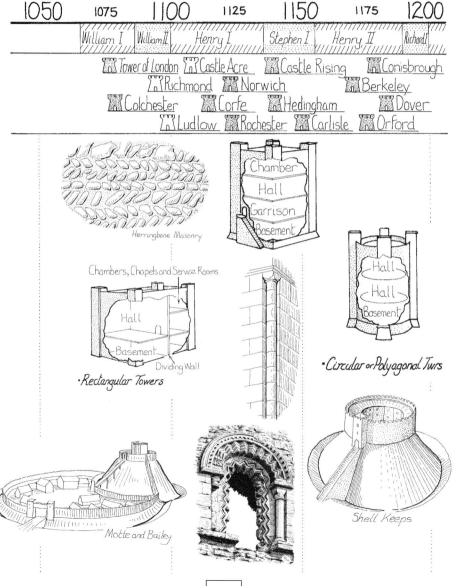

1050	1075	1100	1125	1150	1175	1200

William I | William II | Henry I | Stephen I | Henry II | Richard I

Tower of London · Castle Acre · Castle Rising · Conisbrough
Richmond · Norwich · Berkeley
Colchester · Corfe · Hedingham · Dover
Ludlow · Rochester · Carlisle · Orford

Herringbone Masonry

Chamber
Hall
Garrison
Basement

Chambers, Chapels and Service Rooms

Hall

Basement
Dividing Wall

·*Rectangular Towers*

Hall
Hall
Basement

·*Circular or Polyagonal Turs*

Shell Keeps

Motte and Bailey

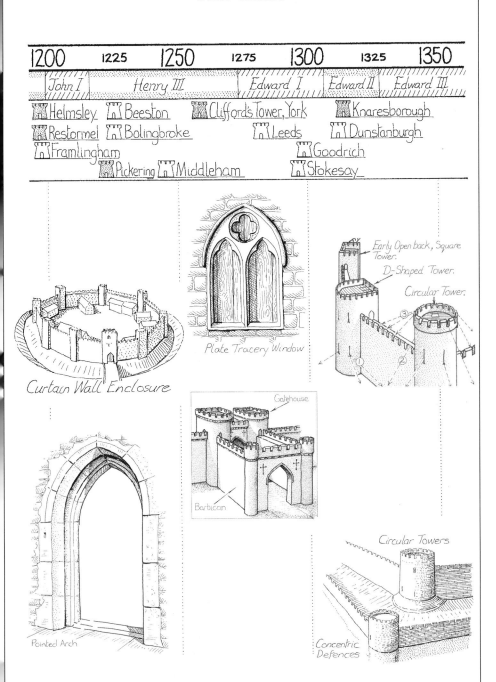

1200	1225	1250	1275	1300	1325	1350

| John I | Henry III | Edward I | Edward II | Edward III |

Helmsley   Beeston   Clifford's Tower, York   Knaresborough
Restormel   Bolingbroke   Leeds   Dunstanburgh
Framlingham   Goodrich
Pickering   Middleham   Stokesay

Curtain Wall Enclosure

Plate Tracery Window

Early Open back, Square Tower.
D-Shaped Tower.
Circular Tower.

Gatehouse

Barbican

Pointed Arch

Circular Towers

Concentric Defences

TIME CHART

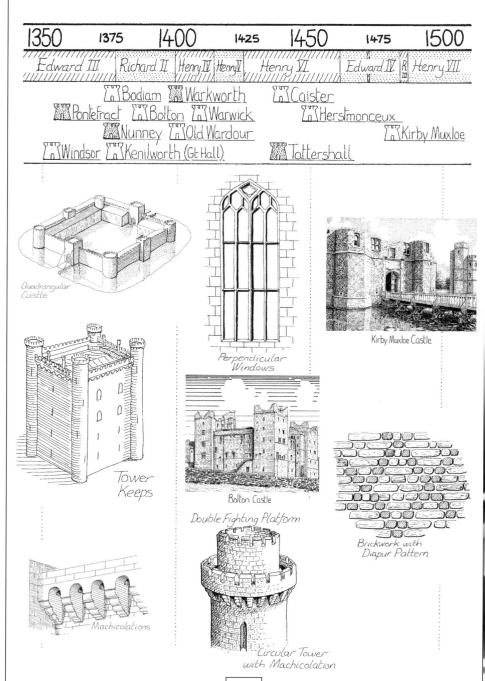

1350	1375	1400	1425	1450	1475	1500
Edward III	Richard II	Henry IV	Henry V	Henry VI	Edward IV	R III	Henry VII

Bodiam　Warkworth　Caister

Pontefract　Bolton　Warwick　Herstmonceux

Nunney　Old Wardour　Kirby Muxloe

Windsor　Kenilworth (Gt Hall)　Tattershall

Quadrangular Castle

Perpendicular Windows

Kirby Muxloe Castle

Tower Keeps

Bolton Castle

Double Fighting Platform

Brickwork with Diapur Pattern

Machicolations

Circular Tower with Machicolation

Norman

William I	*1066–1087*
William II	*1087–1100*
Henry I	*1100–1135*
Stephen	*1135–1154*

Plantagenet

Henry II	*1151–1189*
Richard I	*1189–1199*
John I	*1199–1216*
Henry III	*1216–1272*
Edward I	*1272–1307*
Edward II	*1307–1327*
Edward III	*1327–1377*
Richard II	*1377–1399*

Lancaster

Henry IV	*1399–1413*
Henry V	*1413–1422*
Henry VI	*1422–1471*

[Deposed *1461*, Murdered *1471*]

York

Edward IV	*1461–1483*

[This is correct!]

Edward V	*1483*
Richard III	*1483–1485*

Tudor

Henry VII	*1485–1509*
Henry VIII	*1509–1547*
Edward VI	*1547–1553*
Mary	*1553–1558*
Elizabeth I	*1558–1603*

Stuart

James I	*1603–1625*
Charles I	*1625–1649*
Commonwealth	*1649–1660*
Charles II	*1660–1685*
James II	*1685–1688*

CASTLES TO VISIT

Below are listed some of the castles mentioned in the text, along with a number of other notable sites that are all open to the public. There is first an explanation of abbreviations and then a selection of websites upon which a wider choice of castles may be found.

(EH): English Heritage. The finest collection of medieval castles is maintained by English Heritage. Some are free to enter, for others there is a charge, although if you plan to visit a number of sites then annual membership is good value as it also includes free or reduced entry to properties in Wales and Scotland:
English Heritage, Customer Services Dept, PO Box 569, Swindon, SN2 2YP.
Telephone: 0870 333 1181
Email: customers@english-heritage.org.uk
Web: www.english-heritage.org.uk

(NT): National Trust. Although dominated by country houses there are a number of castles in their hands:
National Trust, PO Box 39, Bromley, Kent, BR1 3XL. Telephone: 0870 458 4000
Email: enquiries@thenationaltrust.org.uk
Web: www.nationaltrust.org.uk

Below I have listed a number of useful websites, which contain more information about these and numerous other castles with their location, opening times and charges:
www.castleuk.net   www.castlexplorer.co.uk
www.theheritagetrail.co.uk   www.castles-abbeys.co.uk
www.castlegate.net

London and South East

BERKHAMSTED CASTLE, Hertfordshire (EH): Remains of 11th century motte and bailey with some later stonework (SP99/08).

BODIAM CASTLE, Sussex (NT): Impressive late 14th century quadrangular castle still surrounded by a water-filled moat (TQ78/25).

DOVER CASTLE, Kent (EH): One of our most important fortresses, centred upon a huge late 12th century castle with many later features up to the Second World War (TR32/41).

HASTINGS CASTLE, Sussex: 11th-13th century stone walling and a gatehouse remain high above the town, the rest was eroded by the sea. May have been the site of William's castle that he established shortly before the battle in 1066 (TQ82/09).

HERSTMONCEUX CASTLE, Sussex: Impressive 15th century moated brick castle, restored in the last century (TQ64/10). Limited opening times.

LEWES CASTLE, Sussex: An early castle which is rare in having two mottes. Notable 14th century barbican (TQ41/10).

PEVENSEY CASTLE, Sussex (EH): The earliest castle built by William the Conqueror, within an old Roman fort. The ruins were refortified in the Second World War (TQ64/04).

HASTINGS CASTLE

ROCHESTER CASTLE, Kent (EH): Huge 12th century keep with an odd round tower in one corner where the earlier square tower was brought down by King John's miners (TQ74/68).

TOWER OF LONDON, London: This most famous of castles is centred upon the 11th century keep known as the White Tower which is surrounded by mainly 13th century outer walls, towers and moat (TQ34/80).

WALLINGFORD, Oxfordshire: An early motte and bailey castle in the north corner of a Saxon burh (defensive town) (SU61/89). Limited access.

WINDSOR, Berkshire: More of a palace today than castle; extensive building done in the early 19th century. Originally a motte with two baileys either side along the hilltop (SU97/77).

The South and South West

ARUNDEL CASTLE, Sussex: Dramatic fortification owing mainly to restoration in the 19th century and it is still a country residence today. Good example of a 12th century shell keep (TQ01/07).

BERKELEY CASTLE, Gloucestershire: Shell keep and outer walls from the 12th century with later buildings within. The site of Edward II's murder (ST68/98).

CARISBROOKE CASTLE, Isle of Wight (EH): 11th century motte and bailey with 12th

CORFE CASTLE

KIRBY MUXLOE CASTLE

century shell keep and stone walling. Notable as a prison for Charles I (SZ48/87).

CORFE CASTLE, Dorset: Impressive ruins of stone keep, outer walls and towers upon hill overlooking a picturesque planned village (SY95/82).

NUNNEY CASTLE, Somerset (EH): 14th century keep with round corner towers set within a water-filled moat (ST73/45).

OLD WARDOUR CASTLE, Wiltshire (EH): Unusual six sided keep dating from the 14th century, with good access to its surviving interior rooms (ST93/26).

RESTORMEL, Cornwall (EH): An impressive shell keep castle built in the 12th century (SX10/61).

SHERBORNE OLD CASTLE, Dorset (EH): A bishop's palace laid out in the early 12th century with much of its stone walls, gatehouse and keep still standing (ST64/16).

East Anglia and East Midlands

CAISTER CASTLE, Norfolk: A 15th century brick castle with notable round tower (TG50/12).

CASTLE ACRE, Norfolk (EH): A late 11th century motte and bailey castle with the remains of a large hall structure within a shell wall on top of the mound (TF81/15).

CASTLE RISING, Norfolk (EH): Magnificent 12th century keep with much of its interior structure still in place, set within earlier ringwork bank and ditch. Notable forebuilding and decoration (TF66/24).

COLCHESTER CASTLE, Essex: The largest keep in England (and one of the earliest). Notable for Roman brick in its wall as it was built on the ruins of a Roman temple (TL99/25).

FRAMLINGHAM CASTLE, Suffolk (EH): This castle mainly comprises a late 12th century curtain wall and you can still walk around its top (TM28/63).

HEDINGHAM CASTLE, Essex: One of the best preserved Norman keeps, notable for the huge single span arch within the hall (TL78/35).

KIRBY MUXLOE CASTLE, Leicestershire (EH): 15th century quadrangular brick castle surrounded by water-filled moat. Work not completed following the execution of Lord Hastings in 1483. (SK52/04).

LINCOLN CASTLE, Lincolnshire: An early motte and bailey (with 2 mottes) which has towers, curtain wall and a gateway surviving (SK97/71).

NORWICH CASTLE, Norfolk: Possibly the largest motte built in England, with an impressive stone keep added in the early 12th century (renovated in the 19th century) (TG23/08).

ORFORD CASTLE, Suffolk (EH): Unusual polygonal keep dating from the 12th century and restored within (TM41/49).

TATTERSHALL CASTLE, Lincolnshire (NT): Five-storey brick keep towers over remains of 15th century castle. The interior is complete with good views from the battlements (TF21/57).

Central, West and North Midlands

BEESTON CASTLE, Cheshire (EH): 13th century walls surround a dramatic hilltop castle (SJ53/59).

BRIDGNORTH CASTLE, Shropshire: The 12th century keep leans over after partial demolition by Cromwell's troops (SO71/92).

CHESTER CASTLE, Cheshire (EH): A tower and curtain walls survive within a later courthouse and barracks complex (SJ40/65).

GOODRICH CASTLE, Hereford and Worcester (EH): Impressive remains of a 12th century keep surrounded by later walls and towers on a rocky outcrop (SO57/19).

KENILWORTH CASTLE, Warwickshire (EH): The largest ruined castle in England. Features include the 12th century keep and the shell of the 14th century hall (SP27/72).

LUDLOW CASTLE, Shropshire: Late 11th century castle with its gatehouse converted into a great tower in the 12th century. Notable round chapel (SO50/74).

PEVERIL CASTLE, Derbyshire (EH): 11th century walling and a later keep stand

BROUGH CASTLE

RICHMOND CASTLE

dramatically upon the crest of a hill overlooking the village of Castleton (SK15/82).

STOKESAY CASTLE, Shropshire (EH): Well-preserved fortified manor house (SO43/81).

TAMWORTH CASTLE, Staffordshire: Shell keep with some fine herringbone masonry in the walls below (SK20/03).

WARWICK CASTLE, Warwickshire: An 11th century motte and bailey castle, although most of what you see today dates from the 14th century (SP28/04).

The North

ALNWICK CASTLE, Northumberland: Although it took its present shape in the 14th century, this palatial home has work dating from the 12th to the 19th century (NU18/13).

BAMBURGH CASTLE, Northumberland: Dramatically positioned castle upon a site occupied since the Iron Age and which is still occupied (NU18/35).

BARNARD CASTLE, County Durham (EH): Impressively sited above the River Tees with 12th and 13th century walls and tower (NZ04/16).

BOLTON CASTLE, North Yorkshire: Imposing 14th century fortified manor house in the form of a quadrangular castle (SE03/91).

BOWES CASTLE, County Durham (EH): Remains of a large keep within an old Roman fort (NY99/13).

BROUGH CASTLE, Cumbria (EH): Features work from the 11th to the 17th centuries, with ruined keep and curtain wall within old Roman fort (NY79/14).

CARLISLE CASTLE, Cumbria (EH): Important border fortification principally dating from 12th century (NY39/56).

CLIFFORD'S TOWER, York (EH): A 13th century shell keep which is the only surviving part of York Castle. Good views over the city from battlements (SE60/51).

CONISBROUGH, South Yorkshire (EH): Late 12th century castle with a round keep that is unique in England (SK51/98).

DUNSTANBURGH CASTLE, Northumberland: Dramatic ruins of a 14th century castle along a 100 ft high crag (NU25/22).

ETAL CASTLE, Northumberland (EH): Remains of a 14th century castle which fell to the Scots as late as 1513 (NT92/39).

MIDDLEHAM CASTLE, North Yorkshire (EH): 12th century keep surrounded by outer quadrangle with work from the 13th to the 15th century. Original motte and bailey stand on a hill to the south (SE12/87).

NORHAM CASTLE, Northumberland (EH): Late 12th century castle, rebuilt after damage caused by the Scots in 1513 (NT90/47).

PICKERING CASTLE, North Yorkshire (EH): A motte and bailey castle from c1100 which had unusually late replacements in stone of some of its features. Good remains of motte and outer walls (SE80/84).

RABY CASTLE, County Durham: This 14th century fortified home built by the Nevilles has been occupied by the same family since 1626 (NZ12/21).

RICHMOND CASTLE, North Yorkshire (EH): Early stone castle with a rare 11th century hall, but dominated by a huge keep with a magnificent view over the town (NZ17/00).

SCARBOROUGH CASTLE, North Yorkshire (EH): 12th century castle on a site used as a fortification since the Bronze Age. Impressive location and barbican (TA05/89).

WARKWORTH CASTLE, Northumberland (EH): An earlier castle was rebuilt in the late 14th century with an unusual and impressive cross-shaped keep (NU24/05).

GLOSSARY

ALLURE: Another name for the wall walk which runs behind the battlements.

APSE: Semi circular extension to a rectangular building; in the case of a castle found on a number of Norman chapels.

ARCADING: A row of columns supporting arches. Blind arcading is when the pattern of arches and columns lie flat upon a wall rather than having openings.

ARROW LOOP: Vertical slits in a wall or merlon for bowmen to fire through. A horizontal part and round or triangular ends could be added to give a better range especially for crossbows.

ASHLAR: Stone blocks which have been finished with squared sides.

AUMBRY: A wall cupboard built into the stone or brick walls.

BAILEY: The enclosure within the outer walls of a castle. Also known as a WARD.

BALLISTA: A siege engine shaped like a huge crossbow which usually fired iron bolts.

BARBICAN: An outward extension of a gateway used to enhance the defence of the entrance.

BARTIZAN: A small turret projecting from the top corner of a wall or tower.

BASTION: A projection like a tower or turret along a wall which is used for defence.

BATTER: The sloping section of masonry at the bottom of a wall or keep.

BATTLEMENTS: The parapet along the top of a wall or tower with regularly spaced openings. Also known as CRENELLATIONS.

BELFRY: A siege tower.

BERM: Flat strip of land between a ditch and a bank, or in a castle between the walls and the moat.

BRATTICE: Wooden platforms usually temporary and projecting from the top of a tower or wall for defenders to fire and drop missiles upon. More commonly known as HOARDS.

BUTTERY: From the word 'butt' and was where the casks of beer and other drinks in use were stored, while the bulk of the stock was held in the cellars. The buttery was under the watchful eye of the butler.

BUTTRESS: A projecting vertical piece of masonry to help support a wall. A thin, flat type is known as a pilaster buttress and was popular on 11th and 12th century keeps.

CASTELLAN: An official in charge of a castle.

CONCENTRIC DEFENSIVE WALLS: A second outer ring of walling.

CONSTABLE: The official who took charge of the castle in his master's absence.

CORBEL: A shaped stone bracket built out of a wall to support usually timber roofs or floors.

CRENEL: A vertical opening along the battlements. Also known as an EMBRASURE.

CRENELLATION: See BATTLEMENTS.

CROSS-WALL: An internal dividing wall within a larger keep which helped support floors and the roof as well as hinder intruders.

CURTAIN WALLS: Intended to describe outer walls consisting of short lengths of wall which appear to hang between closely spaced towers, but now often used to refer to any walls surrounding castle enclosures.

DOG-LEGGED PASSAGE: A narrow corridor with sharp angled turns, usually found leading to GARDEROBES within the thick walls of a keep.

DONJON: Another word for the great tower or keep. (From the French word for 'lordship', as its height dominated the surroundings and represented the owner's power. Also prisoners were often locked up in the donjon and thus is probably the derivation of the word dungeon.)

DRAWBRIDGE: A flat wooden bridge in front of a gatehouse which could be raised on chains to cover the entrance. (Correctly called a *pont levis* or turning bridge.)

DUNGEON: Derived from the word DONJON, which was often the building whose chambers were used to hold prisoners. Medieval castles were rarely fitted with dungeons, they generally appear in the cellars or ground floors of those which were later used as prisons.

EMBRASURE: See CRENEL.

FOREBUILDING: A building which protected the entrance to a keep and usually incorporated the stairs and often a number of small chambers.

GARDEROBE: A medieval toilet.

GUN: Weapon for firing missiles (derived from the word mangonel (qv)).

GUN LOOP: A hole in a wall from which early guns could be fired.

HERRISONS: Lines of pointed stakes bound together in open scissor formation (from the French word for hedgehog).

HOARDING: See BRATTICE.

KEEP: The name commonly used (from the late 16th century) to refer to the great tower or donjon.

LINTEL: A horizontal block along the top of a window or door opening to support the wall above.

MACHICOLATIONS: A stone version of hoarding or bratticing supported on corbels with slots for dropping missiles down onto attackers.

MANGONEL: A wooden siege engine typically with an arm, one end of which was held in torsion upon the machine's wheeled base while at the other end a cup hurled stones or missiles when the arm was released.

MERLON: The vertical solid part of battlements which stood between the crenels or embrasures.

MOAT: A wide ditch surrounding the outer walls of a castle and usually filled with water. Derived from *motte* the French word for mound.

MOTTE:	The raised, defensive mound upon which a tower and palisade stood, with a bailey below (hence motte and bailey castle).
MURAL GALLERY:	A narrow passage running through the thickness of a wall, often with arched openings looking over the hall.
MURDER HOLES:	Holes in the ceiling of a passageway or gatehouse most likely to have been used for dropping water upon fires lit by attackers in front of wooden doors. Also called *meurtrières*.
NEWEL:	The central column formed by a stone spiral staircase.
ORIEL WINDOW:	A projecting window popular in the 15th and 16th centuries.
OUBLIETTE:	A small chamber accessed by a trapdoor in which prisoners were held.
PALISADE:	A wall made from vertical timbers.
PANTRY:	From the Latin word for bread *panis*, and was originally where the grain was stored although tableware was also kept here. The pantry was the responsibility of the pantler.
PELE TOWER:	Enclosure with reinforced walls, with the defended area known as a 'pele' (from *pilum*, Latin for a stake or palisade). During the 14th and 15th century, towers were erected within them, some in timber but the finest in stone.
PENTISE:	A passage with a sloping roof up against the wall of a building, often between the hall and kitchen in a castle. Also a pentise, or penthouse, was one of the names for the protective roof over a battering ram.
PORTCULLIS:	A wood and iron grid that could be lowered down on chains in front of or behind a doorway. From the Old French *porte-coleice*, meaning sliding door.
POSTERN GATE:	A gateway, typically small and sited to the rear or side of the outer walls of a castle, which could be used as an escape route or back entrance (see also SALLY PORT).
PUTLOG HOLE:	A small socket in a stone wall where horizontal timber scaffold poles were fixed during construction.
QUOIN:	The finished stones that make the corner of a building.
REVETTING:	A stone or timber facing of an earth mound or bank, to give it strength and protect it from the elements. Many early mottes may have been finished this way although all traces have vanished today.
RUBBLE:	Rough stones set in mortar to make the core of many castle walls.
SALLY PORT:	A smaller door fitted within the main gate, or anywhere in the walls of a castle, from which the army would sally forth to attack (see also POSTERN GATE).
SLIGHTING:	To damage a castle in such a way as to render it undefendable.
SOLAR:	A private chamber for the castle owner on an upper floor and accessible from the great hall. More typically associated with

medieval houses, as in a castle the main private room is usually refered to as the great chamber.

SQUINT: A hole in a wall through which to view events in the next room. Usually found in chapel walls.

STEWARD: Man responsible for running the estate and feeding the household in the absence of the lord (from the word 'sty-ward', the man responsible for the pigs).

TREBUCHET: A siege engine that slung stones and missiles via an arm with a counterweight at the opposite end. More accurate and powerful than the earlier mangonel (qv) and is believed to have been used first by Prince Louis in England in 1216.

WALL WALK: The stone path that runs along the top of a wall behind the battlements.

WARD: See BAILEY.

WING WALL: A wall running down the slope of a motte.

BIBLIOGRAPHY

General Castle Books
R. Allen Brown *Castles*
Tim Copeland *Using Castles (A Teachers' Guide)*
Richard Dargie *Castle Under Siege*
Paul Johnson *Castles of England, Scotland and Wales*
Tony McAleavy *Life in a Medieval Castle*
Francois Matarasso *The English Castle*
Plantagenet Somerset Fry *Castles of the British Isles*
Philip Warner *The Medieval Castle: Life in a Fortress in Peace and War*

Guide Books
I also used the guide books to the following castles:
Castle Rising, Clifford's Tower, Colchester, Framlingham and Orford, Goodrich, Kenilworth, Middleham, Morton Corbet, Old Wardour, Peveril, Powis, Richmond, Sherborne Old Castle, Tattershall, the Tower of London, Windsor.

History and Architecture Books
Anthony Alcock *A Short History of Europe*
R.W. Brunskill *Brick Building in Britain*
Jacqueline Fearn *Discovering Heraldry*
John Fleming, Hugh Honour and Nikolaus Pevsner *The Penguin Dictionary of Architecture and Landscape Architecture*
Robert Fossier *The Cambridge Illustrated History of the Middle Ages*
Antonia Fraser (Ed) *The Lives of the Kings and Queens of England*
Trevor Rowley *Norman England*
Christopher Taylor *Parks and Gardens of Britain*

INDEX